EXAMINING PROCEDURES REGARDING PUERTO RICO'S POLITICAL STATUS AND ECONOMIC OUTLOOK

OVERSIGHT HEARING

BEFORE THE

SUBCOMMITTEE ON INDIAN, INSULAR AND ALASKA NATIVE AFFAIRS

OF THE

COMMITTEE ON NATURAL RESOURCES U.S. HOUSE OF REPRESENTATIVES

ONE HUNDRED FOURTEENTH CONGRESS

FIRST SESSION

Wednesday, June 24, 2015

Serial No. 114–13

Printed for the use of the Committee on Natural Resources

Available via the World Wide Web: http://www.fdsys.gov
or
Committee address: http://naturalresources.house.gov

U.S. GOVERNMENT PUBLISHING OFFICE

95–300 PDF   WASHINGTON : 2015

CONTENTS

OVERSIGHT HEARING ON EXAMINING PROCEDURES REGARDING PUERTO RICO'S POLITICAL STATUS AND ECONOMIC OUTLOOK

Wednesday, June 24, 2015
U.S. House of Representatives
Subcommittee on Indian, Insular and Alaska Native Affairs
Committee on Natural Resources
Washington, DC

The subcommittee met, pursuant to notice, at 2:24 p.m., in room 1324, Longworth House Office Building, Hon. Don Young [Chairman of the Subcommittee] presiding.

Present: Representatives Young, Benishek, LaMalfa, Radewagen; Ruiz, Bordallo, Sablan, Pierluisi, and Torres.

Also present: Representatives Serrano and Grijalva.

Mr. YOUNG. The committee will come to order. I do apologize for the delay. Strange as the Congress may be, we have burning questions and we had to talk about the baseball game. They already knew who won and who lost, but then it was beside the point.

Anyway, the Subcommittee on Indian, Insular, and Alaska Native Affairs will come to order. The subcommittee is meeting today to hear testimony on the following oversight topic: "Examining Procedures Regarding Puerto Rico's Political Status and Economic Outlook."

Under Rule 4(f), any oral statements on the hearing are limited to the Chairman and the Ranking Minority Member, and this allows us to hear from the witnesses. We do have two panels here today. Therefore, I ask unanimous consent that all Members' opening statements be made part of the hearing record if they are submitted to the Subcommittee clerk by 5:00 p.m. today, or at the close of the hearing, whichever comes first.

[No response.]

Mr. YOUNG. Hearing no objections, so ordered.

I also ask unanimous consent that the gentleman from New York, Mr. Serrano, be allowed to join us on the dais to be recognized and participate in today's hearing.

[No response.]

Mr. YOUNG. Hearing no objection, so ordered.

STATEMENT OF HON. DON YOUNG, A REPRESENTATIVE IN CONGRESS FROM THE STATE OF ALASKA

Mr. YOUNG. Some time around the turn of this last century, over 100 years ago, John Green Brady, the fifth territorial governor for the District of Alaska, before Alaska was even a territory, was reflecting upon the vain struggle of Alaskans to obtain more initial self-government. The struggle of those Alaskans had lasted for nearly 40 years up to that point, leaving Governor Brady to remark, "We are graduates of the school of patience."

Even today the words of Governor Brady still ring true when referring to American citizens who call the island of Puerto Rico home.

While the plight of Alaska being charted from its humble beginnings as a Department in 1867 to its progression as a District, then as a Territory, then ultimately its admission as the 49th state of the Union in 1959, the overall journey that citizens had to endure lasted for roughly 92 years.

For the past 117 years, another clock has been keeping time on the relationship between the United States and an exotic land off its shores, that of the island of Puerto Rico. Since 1898, the United States of America has held in its possession the island of Puerto Rico.

Since establishing self-governance with the passage of the Federal Relations Act of 1950 and the ratification of the Puerto Rican Constitution in 1952, the United States has allowed Puerto Ricans to govern themselves on internal matters. However, Congress has maintained plenary powers over the islands through the territorial clauses of the U.S. Constitution, Article IV, Section 3, Clause 2.

Today's hearing will aim to continue the discussion on the issue of Puerto Rico's political status, an important discussion given the current economic crisis the island faces today.

For the last 8 years, the island's economy has been mired by recession, a result of misguided management policies from within the public utilities and irresponsible debt trading practices.

As Puerto Rico struggles to solve an economic and financial crisis that is causing a migration of residents off the island to the mainland, Congress must consider how the island's unresolved political status is related to its economic and fiscal problems, and what legislative measures are necessary to restore Puerto Rico's financial stability.

The discussion of political status for the island always sparks lively debate from Puerto Rico and among my colleagues here in Congress and on this committee. I anticipate the same here today, and I welcome it; such spirited debate is healthy.

Holding hearings such as this will further the discussion and drive the point home that Congress maintains its duty to serve the Americans of the island, just as we do to the Americans here on the mainland. We must show the 3.7 million Americans living in Puerto Rico that although they may not have voting representation in the House or the Senate, those of us tending this Nation will hear them when they speak. It is our duty and we honor that duty to listen today.

On a personal level, I have been involved in this project since 1994. I believe very strongly, right up front with you, in statehood. That is no hidden secret. But that is up to the decision of the Puerto Rican people. But the status quo cannot exist—the unfairness to Americans not being listened to by this Congress, and I think the responsibility to the people of Puerto Rico.

A little history about this. Puerto Rico was supposed to become a state first, and Alaska slipped in. I apologize for that. We did a good job.

[Laughter.]

Mr. YOUNG. Then the next was supposed to be Puerto Rico, and it became Hawaii. Puerto Rico is still waiting, 117 years later, to be recognized with full rights, as Americans—not being punished, not being set aside and have higher health rates and, really, frankly, putting a great group of Americans that fought in more wars per capita than any other group of people from any other state.

It is my goal, and always has been, to make a decision. The status quo today will not work. Some will disagree with me, and I know that, and you have your right to that disagreement. But I know what is occurring does not work. The out-migration of what I call the more talented people in Puerto Rico into the mainland is devastating. So, we have to figure something out in this Congress, and my goal is—frankly, stir the pot up—to get things moving.

I want to congratulate my Resident Commissioner, Mr. Pierluisi. He has done an outstanding job presenting his points of view. I admire his other piece of legislation, Chapter 9, that we have to look at. Every other state has that right, only Puerto Rico does not. And we will discuss that in this legislation.

[The prepared statement of Mr. Young follows:]

PREPARED STATEMENT OF THE HON. DON YOUNG, CHAIRMAN, SUBCOMMITTEE ON INDIAN, INSULAR, AND ALASKA NATIVE AFFAIRS

Sometime around the turn of the last century, over 100 years ago, John Green Brady, the fifth territorial governor of the District of Alaska, before Alaska was even a territory, was reflecting upon the vain struggle of Alaskans to obtain more initial self-government.

The struggle of those Alaskans had lasted for nearly 40 years up to that point, leaving Governor Brady to remark, "We are graduates of the school of patience."

Even today the words of Governor Brady still ring true when referring to the American citizens who call the island of Puerto Rico home.

While the plight of Alaska can be charted from its humble beginnings as a Department in 1867 to its progression as a District, then to a Territory and then ultimately to its admission as the 49th state of the Union in 1959, the overall journey its citizens had to endure lasted for roughly 92 years. For the past 117 years, another clock has been keeping time on the relationship between the United States and an exotic land off its shores—that of the island of Puerto Rico. Since 1898, the United States of America has held in its possession the island of Puerto Rico.

Since establishing self-governance through the passage of the Federal Relations Act of 1950 and the ratification of the Puerto Rican Constitution in 1952, the United States has allowed Puerto Ricans to govern themselves on internal matters; however, Congress has maintained plenary powers over the island through the Territorial Clause of the U.S. Constitution, Article IV, Section 3, Clause 2.

Today's hearing will aim to continue the discussion on the issue of Puerto Rico's political status, an important discussion given the current economic crisis the island finds itself in.

For the last 8 years, the island and its economy have been mired by recession, a result of misguided management policies from within the public utilities and irresponsible debt trading practices.

As Puerto Rico struggles to solve an economic and fiscal crisis that is causing a migration of residents to the mainland, Congress must consider how the island's unresolved political status is related to its economic and fiscal troubles, and what legislative measures are necessary to restore Puerto Rico's financial stability.

A discussion of political status for the island always sparks lively debate from within Puerto Rico and among my colleagues here in Congress and on the committee. I anticipate the same here today, and I welcome it—such spirited debate is healthy.

Holding hearings such as this will further the discussion and drive the point home that Congress maintains its duty to serve the Americans of the island just as we do the Americans here on the mainland.

We must show the 3.7 million Americans living in Puerto Rico, from San Juan to Guayama, that although they may not have voting representation in the House or in the Senate, those of us attending today's hearing still hear them when they speak. It is our duty and we honor that duty here today.

————

Mr. YOUNG. With that, I will recognize the Minority Member.

STATEMENT OF THE HON. GREGORIO SABLAN, A DELEGATE IN CONGRESS FROM THE TERRITORY OF THE NORTHERN MARIANA ISLANDS

Mr. SABLAN. Thank you very much, Mr. Chairman. And buenos tardes, everyone. I apologize that it took me, from the Northern Marianas, a little over 500 years before we—I got to see my fellow people from Puerto Rico. At one time we all owed allegiance to a queen. It has been a long time after that allegiance to the queen that you became a part of the United States.

I want to begin by welcoming the witnesses to the hearing, particularly those who traveled from the Island of Puerto Rico to be with us today. I also want to recognize my good friend and colleague, Ms. Gutierrez from Illinois. And I think I saw Ms. Nydia Velazquez here earlier.

I want to especially welcome the leaders of Puerto Rico's three major political parties, as well as our former Natural Resources Committee colleagues, Congressmen and former governors, Luis Fortuño, Aníbal Acevedo Vilá, and Carlos Romero Barceló.

Today's hearing will examine the link between the current economic conditions on Puerto Rico and the unresolved issue of the island's political status. I believe such an examination is fitting, given the severe fiscal difficulties the island is facing.

Currently, the government of Puerto Rico is $73 billion in debt, and there are real concerns that the central government, or one of its instrumentalities, may soon default on its bond payment.

I am from the Northern Mariana Islands, which is a commonwealth that has a permanent relationship with the United States. When Puerto Rico becomes a state, we are next in line, because we start first with the commonwealths, and then we do the others. That is a joke, OK? It is a joke. We have to lighten up the room.

[Laughter.]

Mr. SABLAN. But that makes sense. The commonwealth status in the Marianas was derived from looking at the Puerto Rico status model. Puerto Rico and the Northern Marianas have a long history, like I have alluded earlier. We were a part of Spain, just prior to the Spanish-American War.

But prior to the covenant approval between the United States and the Northern Mariana Islands, the political status commission had to decide the future political status for all the people of the Northern Mariana Islands. And this was no easy feat for a group of Pacific Islanders who had been colonies for hundreds of years, and by an act of political self-determination, we chose a permanent relationship with the United States.

We also had a plebiscite to decide whether we wanted to vote for commonwealth status or reject it with the caveat to participate in the determination of an alternative future political status. We had one. Puerto Rico will have five or six to reach that decision.

I strongly believe that the people of Puerto Rico should similarly be given the opportunity to exercise their right to establish a permanent, unalterable relationship with the United States, or to become an independent country, controlling their own political and economic affairs.

Puerto Ricans have voted in at least five plebiscites since they ratified their local constitution in 1952. The most recent in 2012 saw statehood winning a majority for the first time. In view of this result, which saw statehood receiving 62 percent of the vote and the current status being rejected by 54 percent of voters, my colleague, Congressman Pierluisi, introduced H.R. 727, the Puerto Rico Statehood Admission Process Act.

H.R. 727 would authorize a federally-sponsored vote to be held in Puerto Rico by the end of 2017, with a ballot containing a single question: "Shall Puerto Rico be admitted as a state of the United States"? As a co-sponsor of the Puerto Rico Statehood Admission Act, I am persuaded that the island's territorial status is a cause of its economic conditions.

The unequal treatment in Federal funding currently experienced by Puerto Rico would be transformed into billions of dollars every year under statehood, which would be used to bolster and transform the Puerto Rican local economy for the people of Puerto Rico.

Puerto Rico's status is also the reason its municipalities, such as the Puerto Rico Electric Power Authority, cannot adjust their debts under Chapter 9 of the Federal Bankruptcy Code if they become insolvent. States can choose to allow the municipalities to file for protection under Chapter 9; however, Puerto Rico's government was not authorized to permit its municipalities to seek Chapter 9 bankruptcy relief when Chapter 9 was established by Congress in 1982.

Mr. Chairman, I look forward to working with you to pursue a solution to the unfair and unequal situation that our fellow Americans in Puerto Rico face. It is high time we reached a consensus on a path forward for Puerto Rico to permanently resolve their political status. I thank you, Mr. Chairman.

[The prepared statement of Mr. Sablan follows:]

PREPARED STATEMENT OF THE HON. GREGORIO KILILI CAMACHO SABLAN, A DELEGATE IN CONGRESS FROM THE TERRITORY OF THE NORTHERN MARIANA ISLANDS

Thank you Mr. Chairman. I want to begin by welcoming the witnesses to the hearing, particularly those who traveled from the island of Puerto Rico to be with us today. I want to especially welcome the leaders of Puerto Rico's three major political parties as well as our former Natural Resources Committee colleagues, Congressmen and former governors, Luis Fortuño, Aníbal Acevedo Vilá and Carlos Romero Barceló.

Today's hearing will examine the link between the current economic conditions on Puerto Rico and the unresolved issue of the island's political status. I believe such an examination is fitting given the severe fiscal difficulties the island is facing. Currently the government of Puerto Rico is $73 billion in debt and there are real concerns that the central government or one of its instrumentalities may soon default on its bond payments.

I am from the Northern Mariana Islands, which is a Commonwealth that has a permanent relationship with the United States. The commonwealth status in the Marianas was derived from looking at Puerto Rico's status. Puerto Rico and the Northern Mariana Islands have a long history. We were a part of Spain just prior to the Spanish-American War, but prior to the covenant approval between the United States and the CNMI, the Political Status Commission had to decide the future political status for all the people of the Northern Mariana Islands. This was no easy feat for a group of Pacific Islanders who had been colonies for hundreds of years, and by an act of political self-determination, we chose a permanent relationship with the United States. We also had a plebiscite to decide whether we wanted to vote for commonwealth status or reject it with the caveat to participate in the determination of an alternative future political status.

I strongly believe that the people of Puerto Rico should similarly be given the opportunity to exercise their right to establish a permanent unalterable relationship with the United States or to become an independent country controlling their own political and economic affairs.

Puerto Ricans have voted in at least five plebiscites since they ratified their local constitution in 1952. The most recent in 2012, saw statehood winning a majority for the first time. In view of this result—which saw statehood receiving 62 percent of the vote and the current status being rejected by 54 percent of voters—my colleague, Congressman Pierluisi introduced H.R. 727, the Puerto Rico Statehood Admission Process Act. H.R. 727 would authorize a federally-sponsored vote to be held in Puerto Rico by the end of 2017, with the ballot containing a single question: "Shall Puerto Rico be admitted as a state of the United States?" As a co-sponsor of the Puerto Rico Statehood Admission Act, I am persuaded that the island's territorial status is a cause of its economic conditions.

The unequal treatment in Federal funding currently experienced by Puerto Rico would be transformed into billions of dollars every year under statehood which would be used to bolster and transform the Puerto Rican local economy.

Puerto Rico's status is also the reason its "municipalities"—such as the Puerto Rico Electric Power Authority, (PREPA)—cannot adjust their debts under Chapter 9 of the Federal Bankruptcy Code if they become insolvent. States can choose to allow its municipalities to file for protection under Chapter 9, however Puerto Rico's government was not authorized to permit its municipalities to seek Chapter 9 bankruptcy relief when Chapter 9 was established by Congress in 1982.

Mr. Chairman, I look forward to working with you to pursue a solution to the unfair and equal situation that our fellow Americans in Puerto Rico face. It is high time that we reach a consensus on a path forward for Puerto Rico to permanently resolve their political status.

Thank you.

Mr. YOUNG. I thank the gentleman. And now, I believe our first panel has been seated.

We have the Honorable Pedro Pierluisi, Resident Commissioner; César Miranda, Attorney General for Puerto Rico; and the Honorable Rubén Berríos, President of the Puerto Rican Independence Party.

Honorable Commissioner, you are up.

STATEMENT OF PEDRO R. PIERLUISI, RESIDENT COMMISSIONER OF PUERTO RICO, PRESIDENTE OF NEW PROGRESSIVE PART (PNP), WASHINGTON, DC

Mr. PIERLUISI. Thank you, Chairman Young, Mr. Ranking Member, and members of the subcommittee. The facts are as follows.

Puerto Rico is a territory. If it does not wish to remain a territory, it can become a state or a sovereign nation, either fully independent or with the compact of free association with the United States. However, if Puerto Rico becomes a sovereign nation, future generations of island residents would not be American citizens.

My constituents have made countless contributions to this Nation in times of peace and war, serving in every military conflict since World War I. Many have made the ultimate sacrifice. When they do, their casket is flown back to this country, draped in the American flag. It takes real patriotism to fight for a nation you love, but one that does not treat you equally.

Puerto Rico has more U.S. citizens than 21 states, but my constituents cannot vote for President, have no Senators, and have a non-voting delegate in the House. Moreover, the Constitution gives Congress license to treat territories worse than states, and Congress often uses that license.

Territory status is the root cause of the crisis in Puerto Rico, because Puerto Rico is treated unequally under Federal programs. It is deprived of critical economic support. To compensate, the Puerto Rico government has borrowed heavily, which helps explain why the government and its instrumentalities have $72 billion in debt. In recent years, 250,000 island residents have relocated to the states, and these numbers are only growing. Once in the states they are entitled to full voting rights, and equal treatment under the law, rights they lack in Puerto Rico.

Let me mention two of the many ways that Puerto Rico's status hurts the quality of life of my constituents. First, Puerto Rico is treated unequally under Medicaid and Medicare. The impact on our healthcare system and on our fiscal health has been severe. Second, Congress has authorized each state government to permit its insolvent municipalities to adjust their debts under Chapter 9 of the Bankruptcy Code, but has not authorized Puerto Rico to do so. Thus, territory status is a significant reason why Puerto Rico has excessive debt, and the sole reason why it lacks a critical tool to manage that debt.

I have introduced bills to give Puerto Rico equal treatment under Federal health programs and Chapter 9. While I appreciate that the governor of Puerto Rico has endorsed these efforts, it is ironic that an anti-statehood administration is seeking state-like treatment for the territory in key policy areas. I seek equal treatment for Puerto Rico in all respects.

If you give us the same rights and responsibilities as our fellow American citizens, and let us rise or fall on our merits, we will rise. But if you continue to treat us like second-class citizens, don't profess to be surprised when we fall.

This is now the predominant view in Puerto Rico. In a 2012 referendum, a majority of voters rejected territory status, and more voters expressed a desire for statehood than any other option. At my initiative, Congress approved funding for a federally-sponsored referendum. Once I have the opportunity, I will use this funding to hold a vote on whether Puerto Rico should be admitted as a state, just like Alaska and Hawaii did. This is logical. Statehood won the 2012 referendum. So we should now vote on statehood, itself.

This is also fair. Those who support statehood can vote yes, and those who oppose it can vote no. This approach has brought support in Congress. I have introduced a bill to authorize a vote in Puerto Rico on whether the territory should be admitted to the Union. If a majority of voters say yes, Puerto Rico would become a state within 5 years. The bill has 109 co-sponsors from 39 states and territories, and more bipartisan backing than 99 percent of bills filed this year. Each co-sponsor refutes the single argument that the United States would not accept Puerto Rico as a state.

Puerto Rico's status is intolerable, and my constituents will no longer tolerate it. We want equality under the American flag, and we will settle for nothing less. Thank you.

[The prepared statement of Mr. Pierluisi follows:]

PREPARED STATEMENT OF THE HON. PEDRO R. PIERLUISI, RESIDENT COMMISSIONER OF PUERTO RICO

Chairman Young, Mr. Ranking Member, and members of the subcommittee: Puerto Rico has been a territory of the United States since 1898. As this committee has made clear many times, if Puerto Rico does not want to remain a territory, it can follow one of two paths. The territory can become a state or it can become a sovereign nation, either fully independent from the United States or with a compact of free association with the United States that either nation can terminate. If Puerto Rico becomes a sovereign nation, future generations of island residents would not be American citizens.

Those are the options: remain a territory, become a state, or become a sovereign nation.

As the members of this committee are aware, residents of Puerto Rico have made countless contributions to this Nation in times of peace and war, serving in every military conflict since World War I. They fight today in Afghanistan and other dangerous locations, side-by-side with young men and women from the states. Many of them have made the ultimate sacrifice in battle. And when they do, their casket is flown back to this country, draped in the American flag.

It takes a special kind of patriotism to fight for a nation that you love, but one that does not treat you equally. Although Puerto Rico is home to more American citizens than 21 states, my constituents cannot vote for president, are not represented in the Senate, and have one non-voting delegate in the House—a position I have held since 2009. Moreover, the Constitution gives Congress a license to treat Puerto Rico worse than the states under Federal law, and Congress often uses that license.

Every informed observer understands that territory status is the root cause of the economic, social and demographic crisis in Puerto Rico that you have been reading about in the newspapers. As the GAO noted in a recent report requested by the former chairman of the full Natural Resources Committee, Puerto Rico is treated unequally under Federal spending and tax credit programs and is therefore deprived of billions of dollars every year that would otherwise flow to our local economy, which—not surprisingly—has been mired in a deep recession. To compensate for the shortfall in Federal funding, the Puerto Rico government has borrowed heavily in the bond market, which is the main reason why the territory government and its instrumentalities have $72 billion in outstanding debt. In the last 4 years alone, upwards of 250,000 island residents have relocated to the states in search of better economic opportunities for themselves and their families, and these staggering numbers are only getting worse. When my constituents arrive in the states, they are entitled to vote for their national leaders and to equal treatment under Federal law—the same rights they were denied while living in Puerto Rico. How any American with a conscience could support this shameful situation is, I confess, beyond my comprehension.

There are many concrete examples of how Puerto Rico's territory status harms the quality of life in Puerto Rico, but allow me to mention just two.

Puerto Rico has always been treated in discriminatory fashion under Federal health programs. This is the result of action or inaction by presidents and Members of Congress, both Democrat and Republican, over many decades. The adverse impact on doctors, hospitals, insurance providers and—most importantly—patients in the territory has been as severe as it was predictable. This disparate treatment has also decimated Puerto Rico's fiscal health, since the territory government must cover the costs of services the Federal Government should be covering—and that it *would* be covering if Puerto Rico were a state. Thus, I have introduced a comprehensive bill to essentially provide Puerto Rico with state-like treatment under Medicaid and Medicare.

Another example—Congress has empowered each state government to authorize its "municipalities" to adjust their debts under Chapter 9 of the Federal Bankruptcy Code if they become insolvent. A state government may choose to allow its municipalities to file for protection under Chapter 9, or it may decline to do so. The power to decide rests with the state government. However, for reasons that are clear to nobody, Congress in 1984 chose not to permit the government of Puerto Rico to authorize its municipalities to seek relief under Chapter 9. In other words, Puerto

Rico's territory status is the primary reason why Puerto Rico has so much debt and is the sole reason why Puerto Rico does not possess a critical tool that could help the island manage this debt. I have introduced a bill in Congress to give Puerto Rico state-like treatment under Chapter 9. It is opposed by a handful of investment firms for specious and self-interested reasons, but otherwise has remarkably broad support.

Now I appreciate that the governor of Puerto Rico has endorsed my legislative initiatives with respect to both Federal health programs and Chapter 9. I will continue to fight alongside him in pursuit of these goals. We both want to help Puerto Rico because we both love Puerto Rico. However, I don't know whether to laugh or cry at the irony of the Governor's anti-statehood administration seeking state-like treatment for Puerto Rico in these and other critical policy areas. The fact is that politicians in Puerto Rico who defend or rationalize our territory status are complicit in the terrible treatment this status brings. That may be a tough statement, but it is a true statement.

What I desire for Puerto Rico is simple. I don't need to resort to tortured legal or policy arguments to explain it. I don't seek special, different or unique treatment. I don't ask to be treated any better than the states, but I won't accept being treated any worse either. I want only for Puerto Rico to be treated equally. Give us the same rights and opportunities as our fellow American citizens, and let us rise or fall based on our own merits. Because I know that we will rise.

To be clear, this is not only my personal view. To the contrary, this is now the predominant view among the Puerto Rico public. In 2012, the government of Puerto Rico sponsored a referendum in which a majority of voters rejected Puerto Rico's current territory status and more voters expressed a desire for statehood than for any other status option, including the current territory status. In the wake of that historic vote, I conveyed the results to you—my colleagues in Congress—and to the Obama administration. I did this because, for a territory to become a state, Congress must approve legislation known as "an admission act" and the President must sign that legislation into law, just like any other bill.

At my initiative, the Obama administration in April 2013 requested—and Congress in January 2014 approved with bipartisan support—an appropriation of $2.5 million to fund the first *federally-sponsored* status referendum in Puerto Rico's history. We wrote the provision, which is contained in Public Law 113–76, so that this funding will remain available until it is used. While the law does not prescribe the exact format of the ballot, leaving those details to the Puerto Rico government, it does require the U.S. Department of Justice to certify that the ballot and voter education materials are consistent with U.S. law and policy. This will ensure that the ballot contains only real status options, as opposed to fanciful proposals.

It is now clear that the governor of Puerto Rico will not use this funding before his term in office ends next year—and I hope the members of this subcommittee will ask the Governor's representative at this hearing why not. When I am in a position to utilize this funding, I will do so without hesitation. My proposal is to use the funding to hold a simple yes-or-no vote on whether Puerto Rico should be admitted as a state. This approach is logical and fair. First, it is deeply rooted in precedent. Alaska and Hawaii each conducted federally-sponsored yes or-no votes prior to statehood. Second, because statehood obtained the most votes in the 2012 referendum, it makes sense to now hold a vote on statehood itself. Third, the format is inclusive. Those who support statehood can vote "yes" and those who oppose it for *any* reason can vote "no." Fourth, the vote would yield a definitive result that nobody could reasonably question. Politicians in Puerto Rico who favor the *status quo* have perfected the dark art of seeking to undermine the legitimacy of any vote they lose; the process I have proposed will make it impossible for them to do so again.

This approach has broad support in Congress. In February, I introduced H.R. 727, the Puerto Rico Statehood Admission Process Act. Consistent with my philosophy, the bill would authorize a federally-sponsored vote to be held in Puerto Rico by the end of 2017, with the ballot containing a single question: "Shall Puerto Rico be admitted as a state of the United States?" To conduct this vote, the Puerto Rico government could use the $2.5 million that Congress already approved in Public Law 113–76. If a majority of voters affirm their desire for admission, the bill provides for an automatic series of steps to occur that would culminate in Puerto Rico's admission as a state in the year 2021.

H.R. 727 is forceful and ambitious, because the days of half-steps and half-measures on this issue are over. Yet the bill already has 109 co-sponsors from 39 states and territories, and more bipartisan support than 99 percent of the nearly 3,000 bills that have been introduced in Congress this year. Co-sponsors include the Chairman and Ranking Member of this subcommittee; 7 of the 12 members of this subcommittee; the Ranking Member of the full committee; all 10 Democrats and 4 Republicans from the critical state of Florida; and a majority of the members of the Congressional Hispanic Caucus. Each co-sponsor helps refute the false and cynical argument that the United States would not accept Puerto Rico as an equal member of the American family. Each co-sponsor endorses the proposition that, if a majority of my constituents confirm in a federally-sanctioned vote that they want Puerto Rico be admitted as a state, then Congress should act to implement that democratically expressed desire on a reasonable but rapid timetable. In my view, this is the only morally acceptable position, and I thank those Members who have taken it. You are on the right side of history.

Chairman Young, thank you for scheduling this hearing and for everything you have done over the years to support Puerto Rico's quest for equality through statehood. I know that one day, not too far off, Puerto Rico will follow in Alaska's footsteps.

———

Mr. YOUNG. Well done. César Miranda, Attorney General of Puerto Rico, you are up.

STATEMENT OF CÉSAR R. MIRANDA RODRÍGUEZ, ATTORNEY GENERAL OF PUERTO RICO, TESTIFYING ON BEHALF OF GOVERNOR ALEJANDRO GARCÍA PADILLA, SAN JUAN, PUERTO RICO

Mr. RODRÍGUEZ. Thank you, Chairman Young.

Mr. YOUNG. Turn that microphone on.

Mr. RODRÍGUEZ. Thank you, Chairman Young, members of the subcommittee. My name is César Miranda, I am the Secretary of Justice of Puerto Rico. I am appearing today representing the Governor of Puerto Rico. I am not representing the Popular Democratic Party, but the Governor in his executive capacity.

We have been invited to discuss an issue over which there is no consensus in Puerto Rico. Puerto Rico's political status is a divisive matter, both in Puerto Rico and in this Congress. I recognize the importance of this historical debate. However, given today's fiscal and economic crisis in Puerto Rico, I prefer to direct my testimony to address other matters of urgent importance to our island.

The fiscal and economic situation in Puerto Rico has reached a tipping point. We are in a state of fiscal emergency, as we have no access to the capital markets, and our public institutions face a liquidity crisis. The situation is truly dire. Puerto Rico has been experiencing an unemployment crisis. Unemployment remains twice that of the mainland, and the loss of employment opportunity has cost an increasing number of residents to move to the mainland. Nearly half of all residents in Puerto Rico qualify for low-income health insurance subsidies, and the average personal income per capita was only $17,000 in Fiscal Year 2013.

Puerto Rico's unprecedented economic difficulties have contributed to rising budget deficits that have turned into large debts. Puerto Rico owes approximately $73 million in debt, and it has no ability to refinance it.

I believe that there are certain issues that this Congress can explore to address Puerto Rico's fiscal crisis and put Puerto Rico on a path of long-term fiscal sustainability.

First, the Congress can approve H.R. 870, which was introduced by Resident Commissioner Pierluisi earlier this year. H.R. 870 would amend the U.S. Bankruptcy Code and extend Chapter 9 to Puerto Rico. Extending Chapter 9 would provide significant benefits to all involved. Chapter 9 would provide a process that is understood by creditors, prospective lenders, and suppliers. It would facilitate market access by offering debtor-in-possession financing. There is no good reason to deny Puerto Rico Chapter 9, in what has been proven time and again to be a vital tool for recovering from dire economic consequences. Detroit is the last of those examples.

Second, Congress can provide Puerto Rico with relief from the Jones Act, which drives up the cost of all goods in Puerto Rico and depresses the Puerto Rican economy. Congress could even grant Puerto Rico a temporary extension of the Jones Act, in order to evaluate its impact on the economy before granting a permanent extension.

Third, Congress needs to fix future reductions in Federal health care funding that will harm Puerto Rico residents. These reductions are not in line with the funding treatment received by the 50 states, and they threaten the health and welfare of Puerto Ricans. It also threatens economic stability. Specifically, I understand that a further reduction will occur when the 2016 Center for Medicaid and Medicare Services rate structure becomes effective. This would cut Medicare funding by 11 percent in Puerto Rico, while increasing by 3 percent in the states on the mainland. This cut will compound the financial difficulty for Puerto Ricans who pay the same Social Security and Medicare taxes as residents.

There are some other examples in which Puerto Rico can be assisted by Congress. There is widespread consensus in Puerto Rico on the approval of H.R. 870 to amend the U.S. Bankruptcy Code. In addition, there is consensus in crafting an extension from the Jones Act, and amending the sunset provisions of certain health care funding.

This basically summarizes my positions regarding my appearance today.

[The prepared statement of Mr. Rodríguez follows:]

PREPARED STATEMENT OF CÉSAR R. MIRANDA RODRÍGUEZ, TESTIFYING ON BEHALF OF GOVERNOR ALEJANDRO GARCÍA PADILLA OF PUERTO RICO

Chairman Young, Ranking Member Ruiz, and members of the subcommittee: My name is César R. Miranda Rodríguez, and I am the Secretary of Justice of Puerto Rico. I am the chief legal officer of Puerto Rico and the chief executive of the Department of Justice (the "DOJ"). Prior to my appointment as Secretary of Justice in January 2014, I served as Chief of Staff under former Governor Sila M. Calderon and in many other posts as a public servant. I am appearing today before this subcommittee representing the Governor of Puerto Rico.

We have been invited today to discuss an issue over which there is no consensus, but quite the opposite either in Puerto Rico or in Congress. The status of Puerto Rico is a debate in which we have been perpetually immersed for well over a century. It has always been a divisive matter in Puerto Rico as in Congress. Recognizing the importance of such a historical debate but taking into consideration the extreme fiscal and economic crisis that we are facing in Puerto Rico, I honestly prefer to direct my participation to address other matters of the utmost importance for our Island, in which there is a common understanding and consensus.

The first of these issues is the approval of H.R. 870, which was introduced by our Resident Commissioner. H.R. 870 would amend the U.S. Bankruptcy Code to treat Puerto Rico like a "state" for purposes of Chapter 9. Its approval is supported among all political parties in Puerto Rico and among informed experts and intellectuals in the United States. In addition to passing H.R. 870, and as I discuss below, there are other uncontroversial measures Congress can take to assist Puerto Rico, including crafting a limited exemption for Puerto Rico from the Jones Act, fixing the automatic sunset provisions of health care funding, and providing much-needed certainty on creditability of certain taxes paid in Puerto Rico. These are just a few of the ways in which Congress can assist Puerto Rico.

ECONOMIC CRISIS IN PUERTO RICO

I would like to begin by emphasizing that the fiscal and economic situation in Puerto Rico has reached a tipping point. The Legislative Assembly has declared a fiscal emergency, the credit markets have closed their doors, and many of Puerto Rico's public institutions face liquidity crises. The situation is truly dire, and it is important to tell why it is so.

Puerto Rico's economy is closely tied to that of the United States but was disproportionately and adversely impacted by the U.S. financial crisis and the "Great Recession." The Commonwealth has experienced high unemployment rates, steady population decline, loss of industry, consecutive budget deficits, and truly unprecedented levels of debt and unfunded pension obligations. A number of significant economic and legal factors have contributed to this fiscal crisis. An example of this is the repeal and phase-out by Congress of Section 936 of the Internal Revenue Code, which, until its phase-out in 2005, provided tax benefits for certain businesses (including large pharmaceutical companies) operating in Puerto Rico. The elimination of these tax benefits led to a significant loss of employment in Puerto Rico's manufacturing sector, and generated strong headwinds for economic growth. Other factors include the decline in the local housing sector, the failure of a number of local banking entities, and the doubling in oil prices between 2005 and 2012 (this posed a major problem for the Commonwealth given its dependence on oil for virtually all of its power generation).

The Commonwealth has also been experiencing an unemployment crisis. In fact, unemployment remained above 15 percent for many years following the financial crisis, suggesting continued weakness in Puerto Rico's economy. Unemployment dropped to a still-elevated rate of 12.1 percent at the end of 2014 while unemployment in the rest of the United States dropped to 5.6 percent. The loss of employment opportunities in the Commonwealth has caused an increasing number of residents to seek opportunities in the mainland. Many residents that are leaving are those with the greatest earnings potential, while many who remain strain existing resources at a time when the Commonwealth is least able to meet such demands. In fact, nearly half of all residents in Puerto Rico qualify for low-income health insurance subsidies, and the average personal income per capita, including transfer payments, was approximately $17,000 in Fiscal Year 2013.

Puerto Rico's unprecedented economic difficulties have contributed to rising budget deficits at all levels of government, including at Puerto Rico's public corporations. Historically, these entities have relied on access to the credit markets, interim financing from the Government Development Bank for Puerto Rico (the "GDB"), and private-sector banks to cover budget shortfalls and provide essential services. Today, these entities have been closed out of the credit markets and are unable to refinance any portion of their nearly $73 billion in outstanding public debt. In addition, Puerto Rico's public pension funds, though subject to a major overhaul during Fiscal Year 2014 that reduced future annual cash-flow needs, still face significant unfunded liabilities, which will require increased governmental contributions in the coming years.

Governor Alejandro García Padilla has taken unprecedented fiscal measures in an effort to achieve long-term fiscal sustainability in Puerto Rico. Within 2 years of taking office, for example, the Padilla administration reduced budget deficits, imposed unprecedented cost-control measures at the central government and public corporation levels, established limits on government payroll (as of November 2014, there were 92,842 government employees, compared to 139,640 in 2008), implemented comprehensive pension reform, imposed loan origination discipline at the GDB, reformed rates at certain public corporations, and completed and is actively exploring public-private partnerships.

One critical component of achieving fiscal sustainability is ensuring that Puerto Rico's governmental instrumentalities are self-sufficient. In Puerto Rico, public services, including water and wastewater services, electric power, and transportation are performed by state-owned public corporations. The most critical public corporations in Puerto Rico are: (1) the Puerto Rico Electric Power Authority (often referred to as "PREPA"), which provides substantially all of the electricity to residents, businesses and governmental units in Puerto Rico; (2) the Puerto Rico Aqueduct and Sewer Authority (often referred to as "PRASA"), which provides 97 percent of the water and 59 percent of the wastewater services to residents in Puerto Rico; and (3) the Puerto Rico Highways and Transportation Authority (often referred to as

"PRHTA"), which is responsible for highway construction and maintenance on the island.

The fact that Puerto Rico is an island exacerbates its already high cost of providing these services. In November 2014, for example, utility customers in Puerto Rico paid more than twice the national average per kilowatt hour for electricity. Nonetheless, these public corporations have had chronic budget deficits in recent years resulting, in part, from population and economic decline. In 2012–2013 alone, the combined deficit of PREPA, PRASA, and PRHTA was over $800 million. Public corporations have historically financed their deficits by relying on capital market financings or the central government, which has provided loans through the GDB or private sector banks. These deficits, combined with borrowings for infrastructure projects, have left these three public corporations with over $20 billion in debt.

PREPA

I would like to provide additional detail on the fiscal crisis at PREPA because it provides an example that illuminates some of the challenges that Puerto Rico faces more generally in the absence of a legal regime like Chapter 9.

PREPA supplies virtually all of the electricity in Puerto Rico and carries a debt burden of over $9 billion, including approximately over $1.1 billion that is due on or before July 1, 2015. PREPA has been facing a financial crisis since the summer of 2014 when nearly $700 million in revolving credit lines was set to expire and PREPA was unable to access the capital markets or secure financing from other sources. In response, the Legislative Assembly adopted the Public Corporation Debt Enforcement and Recovery Act (the "Recovery Act") to provide a framework for a consensual resolution of PREPA's liquidity and debt crisis that would have been negotiated between PREPA and its creditors. Because Puerto Rico is precluded from invoking Chapter 9 of the U.S. Bankruptcy Code, such a measure was seen as vital to bringing the necessary parties to the negotiating table. Following enactment of the Recovery Act, PREPA succeeded in executing forbearance agreements with its revolving credit-line lenders and the insurers and bondholders controlling more than 60 percent of PREPA's $8.3 billion of outstanding power revenue bonds.

The forbearance agreements enabled PREPA to conserve cash, thereby improving its liquidity and stabilizing its operations, while also providing PREPA with much-needed time to develop a long-term recovery plan. Under those agreements, PREPA was authorized to use funds for ordinary operational expenses that would otherwise have been required to pay debt service and was temporarily excused from making hundreds of millions of dollars in payments into reserve accounts for the payment of debt service. PREPA's ongoing ability to operate today is due in large part to the relaxation of these financial obligations during the forbearance period that may not have been possible but for the existence of the Recovery Act. In fact, the forbearance agreements expire at the end of June 2015, and PREPA faces imminent default and an uncertain future beyond June. As the sole provider of electricity in Puerto Rico, this is really not a tenable situation. Unfortunately, many other government entities in Puerto Rico could find themselves in similar positions in the future.

THE RECOVERY ACT

Research and experience makes clear that investors, creditors and anyone doing business in or with Puerto Rico need to have more clarity on how the Commonwealth's financial crisis might be resolved before investing in or transacting business with Puerto Rico. The establishment of an orderly and consensus-based process for addressing outstanding debt at the public corporations is absolutely vital to providing this clarity. Our public corporations are not eligible to reorganize under Chapter 11 of the U.S. Bankruptcy Code because they are governmental units, and they are not eligible to adjust their debts under Chapter 9 because Puerto Rico is expressly—and inexplicably—excluded from the U.S. Bankruptcy Code's definition of "State" for purposes of Chapter 9 eligibility. Prior to the enactment of the Recovery Act in June 2014, Puerto Rico was in the unique position of having no means for authorizing a legal regime under which its public corporations could adjust their debt or address creditor claims in an orderly manner.

The Legislative Assembly's adoption of the Recovery Act in 2014 was a response to the legislative gap in the U.S. Bankruptcy Code. The Recovery Act was designed to allow public corporations to adjust their debt in an orderly process—with creditor input and court supervision—while protecting the collective interest of their constituents, including bondholders and other creditors, as well Puerto Rico's residents and businesses who depend on them for the essential services they provide. The Recovery Act ensured that the provision of essential public services to Puerto Rico's residents would not be interrupted in the event of a fiscal emergency.

Immediately after the passage of the Recovery Act, two groups of PREPA bondholders filed suit, seeking judgments declaring the Recovery Act unconstitutional. On February 6, 2015, the U.S. District Court for the District of Puerto Rico enjoined enforcement of the Recovery Act, holding that the Recovery Act is unconstitutional because it is pre-empted by Section 903 of the U.S. Bankruptcy Code. Specifically, the court concluded that Puerto Rico cannot pass a law allowing its public corporations to adjust their debts through a method of composition. The Commonwealth and the GDB have appealed the ruling and the matter is under advisement. It is not appropriate for me to comment on the specifics of the appeal, or the reasons why we believe the Recovery Act is lawful, but I can say that we are hopeful that the court will uphold the legality of the Recovery Act as a means of addressing Puerto Rico's fiscal crisis.

More recently, the Commonwealth's Resident Commissioner, the Hon. Pedro Pierluisi, who joins me on the panel, introduced legislation that would amend the U.S. Bankruptcy Code's definition of "State" to include Puerto Rico for purposes of Chapter 9. *See* H.R. 870, 114th Cong. § 2 (2015). If enacted, the Commonwealth's political subdivisions, public agencies, and instrumentalities would be treated like every other municipality in the United States. There would no longer be a need for the Recovery Act.

In the end, the practical and unfortunate result of the District Court's decision enjoining enforcement of the Recovery Act is that there is currently no available legal regime for Puerto Rico's public corporations to adjust their debts through a consensus-based, court-supervised process. In this respect, Puerto Rico is treated differently than every state in the Nation.

THE CONSEQUENCES OF TREATING PUERTO RICO DIFFERENTLY UNDER THE BANKRUPTCY CODE ARE SIGNIFICANT, BUT EXTENDING CHAPTER 9 TO PUERTO RICO PROVIDES SIGNIFICANT BENEFITS

The absence of any legislative tools to adjust the debts of Puerto Rico's public corporations has exacerbated Puerto Rico's fiscal challenges by creating an environment of uncertainty that makes it more difficult to address these challenges. It has increased Puerto Rico's cost of borrowing; it may require Puerto Rico to take extraordinary liquidity measures to ensure the continued performance of essential public services; it may encourage creditors to race to the courthouse and exercise remedies that include attempting to appoint a receiver; and it will ultimately depress economic growth in Puerto Rico, making long-term investment and capital expenditure plans at the public corporations impossible.

Extending Chapter 9 to Puerto Rico, however, would provide significant benefits to all stakeholders.

First, Chapter 9 provides an orderly process for debt adjustment that is understood by the capital markets, creditors, prospective lenders, and suppliers. Specifically, it provides a framework that requires the public corporation to negotiate in good faith, creating an ideal environment to reach consensus under the supervision of an experienced court. Chapter 9 has also been tested many times, including, most recently, in Detroit, Michigan, Stockton, California, and Jefferson County, Alabama, to name a few. These municipalities are now on their way to recovery and renewed prosperity.

Second, public corporations in Chapter 9 would be permitted to obtain debtor-in-possession financing and use cash collateral under well-tested procedures, permitting the continuation of normal operations and the provision of essential public services to Puerto Rico's residents. Third, oversight by a U.S. Bankruptcy Judge with expertise in insolvency matters will also ensure that all parties in interest have recourse to an independent arbiter and no party is denied its rights.

In short, the virtue of Chapter 9 can be seen in the successes of its most recent graduates, including the city of Detroit, whose adjustment proceedings lasted less than 18 months, and Stockton, whose adjustment proceedings lasted less than 2 years. There is simply no good reason to deny the residents and creditors of Puerto Rico what has proven time and again to be a vital tool for recovering from dire economic straits.

CONGRESS CAN TAKE OTHER MEASURES TO ASSIST PUERTO RICO IN NAVIGATING THROUGH THIS CRISIS

There are a number of other measures Congress can take to assist Puerto Rico during this financial crisis. For example, Congress could provide Puerto Rico with a limited exemption from the Merchant Marine Act of 1920, which is more commonly known as the "Jones Act," to significantly reduce the cost of doing business and delivery services in Puerto Rico. The Jones Act imposes significant restrictions on shipping between U.S. ports, thereby significantly driving up the cost of all goods in Puerto Rico and depressing the Puerto Rican economy. The Jones Act requires that all goods shipped, or passengers conveyed, by water between ports in the United States, including ports in Puerto Rico, be carried in U.S.-flagged ships, which are primarily constructed in the United States and owned and crewed by U.S. citizens and permanent residents. Because Puerto Rico is an island economy, the Jones Act disproportionately harms the local economy. Specifically, the Jones Act severely limits the supply and increases the costs of shipping services, imposing a substantial burden on local productivity (this is particularly pronounced in Puerto Rico's energy sector—including PREPA—because nearly all of the electricity is generated by oil that is shipped to Puerto Rico). Congress could even grant a temporary exemption from the Jones Act in order to evaluate its impact on Puerto Rico's economy and assess the costs and benefits of a permanent exemption.

Moreover, Congress needs to fix the significant reductions in Federal health care funding that will harm Puerto Rico's residents in the near future. Puerto Rico has begun experiencing significant reductions in Federal health care funding. These reductions are not in line with funding treatment received by the 50 states and they threaten the health and welfare of Puerto Ricans, as well as Puerto Rico's financial and economic stability. I understand that a further reduction will occur when the 2016 Center for Medicaid and Medicare Services rate structure becomes effective and cuts Medicare Advantage funding by 11 percent in Puerto Rico while increasing it by 3 percent on the mainland. This cut compounds the difficulties that Puerto Ricans—who pay the same Social Security and Medicare taxes as mainland residents, but receive significantly lower reimbursement rates—face. It also threatens the viability of Medicare Advantage on a going-forward basis, and should Medicare Advantage collapse, patients may move to Mi Salud, Puerto Rico's Medicaid program, which already receives 70 percent lower reimbursement rates than any mainland state and faces a funding shortfall within the next few years, when a grant provided under the Affordable Care Act is exhausted.

Finally, Congress and the U.S. Department of the Treasury can provide clarity on the creditability of certain taxes paid in Puerto Rico pursuant to a local law known as Act 154 on Federal income tax returns. Act 154, which was enacted in 2010, imposed a special temporary excise tax and has become one of Puerto Rico's principal sources of tax revenue. Act 154 revenues accounted for approximately 20 percent of Puerto Rico's General Fund revenues in 2012, 2013, and 2014. The Act 154 tax base is very small (only 27 groups of affiliated taxpayers paid the special temporary excise tax in Fiscal Year 2015), and six of these groups accounted for approximately 75 percent of collections. The GDB has noted that any action the U.S. Department of the Treasury to reduce or eliminate the Federal income tax credit available with respect to the Act 154 temporary excise tax is likely to reduce Act 154 revenues.

In conclusion, I believe that we should focus our attention to these matters of critical importance to our Island, around which there is common understanding and consensus. There is widespread consensus on the approval of H.R. 870, which was introduced by our Resident Commissioner, to amend the U.S. Bankruptcy Code to treat Puerto Rico like a "state" for purposes of Chapter 9. In addition, Congress can take other measures, including crafting an exemption from the Jones Act, amending the automatic sunset provisions of much-needed health care funding, and providing certainty on creditability of certain taxes paid in Puerto Rico. Of course, these are just a few of the ways in which Congress can assist Puerto Rico, but they would be a good start.

———

Mr. YOUNG. Thank you, sir. Rubén Berríos, former Senator, Puerto Rican Senate Independence Party, you are up.

STATEMENT OF RUBÉN BERRÍOS, FORMER SENATOR IN THE PUERTO RICAN SENATE, PRESIDENT OF THE PUERTO RICO INDEPENDENCE PARTY (PIP), SAN JUAN, PUERTO RICO

Mr. BERRÍOS. Mr. Chairman and members of the subcommittee, the virtual bankruptcy of Puerto Rico's economy is a self-evident reality. Puerto Rican voters have repudiated the territorial status that is the root cause of our economic and social problems. The territorial status was never democratic and has now become tyrannical.

Internationally, the community of Latin American and Caribbean states has recently reaffirmed its support for the right of Puerto Rico to its self-determination and independence. And yet Congress refuses to comply with its decolonizing obligation toward Puerto Rico.

This subcommittee is well aware of Puerto Rico's status problem. For decades it has held hearings on the issue, and many in Puerto Rico can reasonably wonder whether this oversight hearing pursues a legitimate legislative purpose, or is merely a pro forma, partisan, quid pro quo. Only time will tell.

I shall utilize this hearing to publicly propose a route map toward the solution of Puerto Rico's status problem. The relationship between Puerto Rico's territorial status and our economic and social problems has been well summarized by Senator Ron Wyden, Chairman of the Committee on Energy and Natural Resources. I quote, "Puerto Rico faces huge economic and social challenges. . . . The lack of resolution of Puerto Rico's status not only distracts from addressing these and other issues, it contributes to them. As the most recent reports from the President's Task Force on Puerto Rico's status found—and I quote—'identifying the most effective means of assisting the Puerto Rican economy depends on resolving the ultimate question of status'."

Senator Wyden further added, "The present relationship undermines our moral position in the world."

To say that Puerto Rico should first decide what it wants, as President Obama has proposed, is merely an excuse to evade the legal responsibility of the United States as a colonial power, particularly when the President insists that the territorial relationship already repudiated by the Puerto Rican electorate should be one of the options. Colonialism is the problem, not the solution.

We, therefore, propose the following process to resolve Puerto Rico's status problem. Puerto Rico and the U.S. Congress should engage in a collaborative process of self-determination for Puerto Rico.

In Puerto Rico, various proposals have been advanced to initiate the process. The party I preside, for example, has proposed a status assembly in which each status option, proportionately represented, would formulate a proposal for its desired non-colonial, non-territorial option, requiring a response by the U.S. Government by a date certain. Ultimately, only realistic, non-territorial options negotiated with the U.S. authorities would be submitted to the Puerto Rican electorate.

Unfortunately, the present government of Puerto Rico refuses to move in this direction. However, Congress could jump start a process directed toward the same end. Bipartisan representatives of the congressional leadership, in coordination with the executive branch, could convene representatives of the different status alternatives to present their respective decolonizing status proposals. In response, Congress would then specify which alternatives, and under what conditions it would be willing to consider. The Puerto Rican people could then cast a meaningful vote for the available non-colonial, non-territorial options.

If Congress takes no action, and the colonialist PPD prevails in Puerto Rico's 2016 election, the democratic bankrupt territory of extreme dependency will continue to breed support for statehood. If the pro-statehood party prevails, Congress will then be faced with a statehood petition as a consequence of a statehood yes-or-no vote. That vote would be totally uninformed as to the conditions that Congress would impose, and driven principally by the widespread notion that statehood represents an endless cornucopia of Federal funds. You would then be faced not only with the economic crisis in Puerto Rico, but with a political crisis of unforeseeable consequences to the United States. The rational way to avoid such a scenario would be to start a collaborative process of self-determination.

Time is running out. To conclude, I must urge and demand of the President of the United States the immediate release of political prisoner Oscar López Rivera, who has been in prison for more than 34 years here in the United States. Thank you very much.

[The prepared statement of Mr. Berríos follows:]

PREPARED STATEMENT OF RUBÉN BERRÍOS MARTÍNEZ, PRESIDENT, PUERTO RICAN INDEPENDENCE PARTY

Mr. Chairman and members of the subcommittee: The virtual bankruptcy of Puerto Rico's economy is a self-evident reality.

Puerto Rican voters have repudiated the territorial status that is the root cause of our economic and social problems. A territorial status that was never democratic has now become tyrannical.

Internationally the community of Latin American and Caribbean states (CELAC) which includes all the heads of states of the region has recently reaffirmed its support for the right of Puerto Rico to its self-determination and independence. A similar position has been adopted by the U.N. Decolonization Committee.

And yet Congress refuses to comply with its decolonizing obligation toward Puerto Rico.

What more is needed for Congress to act?

It is my duty as President of the Puerto Rican Independence Party to utilize any forum available to demand an end to colonial rule. Furthermore I shall utilize this hearing to publicly propose a route map toward the solution of Puerto Rico's status problem.

The relationship between Puerto Rico's territorial status and our economic and social problems is by now a recognized reality. In the words of Senator Ron Wyden, Chairman of the Committee on Energy and Natural Resources at an oversight hearing on August 1, 2013, "Puerto Rico faces huge economic and social challenges. Per capita income is stuck at about half that the poorest U.S. state. The violent crime rate is well above the national average and raising. The lack of resolution of Puerto Rico's status, *not only distracts from addressing these and other issues, it contributes to them.* As the most recent reports from the president's Task Force on Puerto Rico's status found and I quote, *"identifying the most effective means of assisting the Puerto Rican economy depends on resolving the ultimate question of status".*" [The emphasis is mine]

The real question before Congress is therefore what will you do to bring about a resolution to Puerto Rico's undemocratic political subordination?

To say that Puerto Rico should first decide what it wants, as President Obama has proposed, is merely an excuse to evade the legal obligations of the United States as a colonial power; particularly when the President insists that the territorial relationship—already repudiated by the Puerto Rican electorate—should be one of the options. Colonialism is the problem, not the solution.

Furthermore for there to be a meaningful choice among viable alternatives, the U.S. Government must clarify what the decolonizing options are, what each would entail, and under what conditions it would commit to a process to achieve them.

We therefore propose the following process to resolve Puerto Rico's status problem: *Puerto Rico and the U.S. Congress should engage in a Collaborative Procedure for the Self-Determination of Puerto Rico.*

It is the rational way out.

In Puerto Rico various proposals have been advanced to initiate the process. The party I preside, for example, has proposed a Status Assembly in which each status option proportionately represented would formulate a proposal for its desired non-colonial, non-territorial option requiring a response by the U.S. Government by a date certain. In the demand for a response all delegations would stand united. Ultimately only realistic non-territorial options negotiated with U.S. authorities would be submitted to the Puerto Rican electorate.

Unfortunately the present government of Puerto Rico refuses to move in this direction.

However, Congress could jump start a process directed toward the same end. An appropriate mechanism could be established to operate within a limited time frame. Bipartisan representatives of the congressional leadership in coordination with the executive branch would convene representatives of the different status alternatives to present their respective decolonizing status proposals. In response Congress would then specify which alternatives and under what conditions it would be willing to consider. The Puerto Rican people could then cast a meaningful vote for the available non-colonial, non-territorial options. Naturally any alternative other than independence involves a process of mutual self-determination.

If Congress takes no action and the colonialist PPD prevails in Puerto Rico's 2016 election, the undemocratic bankrupt territory of extreme dependency will continue to breed support for statehood. If the pro-statehood PNP prevails Congress will then be faced with a statehood petition as a consequence of a Statehood Yes or No vote which that party has pledged to implement. That vote would be totally uninformed as to the conditions that Congress would impose and driven principally by the widespread notion that statehood represents an endless cornucopia of Federal funds. You would then be faced not only with an economic crisis in Puerto Rico, but with a political crisis of unforeseeable consequences in the United States. The rational way to avoid such a scenario would be to start a Collaborative Process of Self-determination.

The choice is yours. Time is running out.

I have included an addendum which is a detailed exposition of the relationship between Puerto Rico's territorial status and our economic and social problems.

Addendum

La economía de Estados Unidos ha estado creciendo, luego de la crisis de 2008, desde el tercer trimestre del año 2009. Su desempleo, que llegó hasta un 10 por ciento, se ubica en alrededor de 5.5 por ciento. En contraste, la economía de Puerto Rico, cuya "recesión" se inició oficialmente en marzo de 2006 –antes de la crisis financiera de Estados Unidos y de otros países- continúa en franca contracción. Este desfase entre Puerto Rico y Estados Unidos hace patente el hecho de que el agotamiento de la economía de nuestro país no es un fenómeno cíclico o pasajero sino que, como han señalado tantos economistas del patio como extranjeros (entre otros el premio Nobel de Economía Joseph Stiglitz), se trata de un problema estructural e institucional.

En síntesis, Puerto Rico carece de los instrumentos institucionales (fiscales, monetarios, comerciales, regulatorios, etc.) para desarrollarse sanamente. Por lo tanto, ante la crisis lo único que hace es manifestar su impotencia.

Los titulares de los periódicos destacan diariamente la indefensión política, la contracción económica, el descalabro social, el peso del endeudamiento y la insuficiencia fiscal del gobierno. Ya los hechos son más elocuentes que las palabras.

Del año 2006 al presente la ruta que ha transitado la economía de Puerto Rico solo puede caracterizarse como catastrófica. Según los datos de la Junta de Planificación el Producto Nacional Bruto sobre bases reales se ha reducido en más de 13 por ciento. Esta contracción se refleja dramáticamente en el mercado de empleo. Del año fiscal 2006 al año fiscal 2014 el número de personas empleadas se redujo en 20 por ciento. Puerto Rico cuenta con una de las tasas de empleo –la proporción de empleados respecto a la población de 16 años o más- más baja del mundo. En el año 2006 era de 43.2 por ciento. Eso es bajo. Hoy no sobrepasa el 35 por ciento. En otras palabras, el 65 por ciento de la población de 16 años o más no está empleada. Esto, aparte del desempleo, se traduce en dos grandes problemas: dependencia y desarrollo de la economía informal o subterránea, con el consecuente azote de la criminalidad y de la creciente inseguridad social que todo esto genera.

Estos problemas no deben despacharse como si fueran expresión de una fase pasajera del mercado o reflejo de la crisis financiera en otros países. La contracción económica comenzó en marzo de 2006 –hace nueve años-, mucho antes que la debacle financiera que precipitara la recesión en la economía estadounidense y en otras economías. Además, fue precedida por un largo periodo de relativo estancamiento, a partir de la década de 1970, que ni la Sección 936, ni las transferencias Federales ni el endeudamiento público pudieron evitar. A este periodo le precedió un tramo de alto crecimiento del enclave industrial en función de privilegios fiscales que no pudo conjurar los altos niveles de desempleo y que se acompañó de un enorme flujo emigratorio y de una creciente remisión de ganancias hacia el exterior.

En el siglo 21 la emigración masiva ha reaparecido con mayor intensidad, hasta el extremo que la población total del país acusa reducción continua. Por otro lado, aunque resulte inconcebible, los rendimientos de capital (ganancias, dividendos e intereses) remitidos al exterior sumaron $36,052.2 millones en el año fiscal 2014. Esto refleja una mezcla perversa de exenciones tributarias y precios de transferencia que han permitido la instalación de enclaves económicos cuyos beneficios no se traducen en desarrollo sustentable para el país.

Ahora, la agudización de todos los problemas citados coincide con un gobierno cuyos grados de libertad de operación parecen reducidos al mínimo: sus finanzas "agonizan" y su margen de endeudamiento ha llegado prácticamente al límite. El escenario fiscal luce trágico: déficit presupuestario, deuda insostenible, anuncio de recortes, inseguridad de empleo, deterioro de servicios, impuestos improvisados, sistemas de retiro en crisis, medidas de corto plazo (como la transferencia de fondos del Fondo del Seguro del Estado al Fondo General) que agravarían la situación en el futuro inmediato y sume y siga. Y todo esto acompañado por un sector corporativo público, encabezado por la Autoridad de Energía Eléctrica, igualmente lastrado por deudas e insolvencia.

Ante tal panorama económico aún los defensores de la colonia han reconocido que hay que realizar reformas institucionales, como es el caso, por ejemplo, de las Leyes de Cabotaje y la Ley de Quiebras donde se hace patente el hecho de que Puerto Rico es una colonia. Pero para superar los graves problemas que Puerto Rico enfrenta no basta con reformar una que otra ley. Puerto Rico necesita una completa caja de herramientas políticas y económicas para llevar a cabo los profundos cambios institucionales y estructurales que le permitan encarar sus problemas efectivamente. La condición indispensable para la articulación del nuevo ordenamiento institucional es pues, la superación del coloniaje a través de la independencia que es la única que provee la caja de herramientas que necesitamos.

Vivimos en un mundo en el que los cambios institucionales y tecnológicos se han acelerado. Estamos rodeados de nuevos arreglos políticos y de nuevas redes de relaciones económicas cobijadas por complejos tratados multilaterales, regionales y bilaterales. Puerto Rico no puede permanecer al margen. Le va la vida.

La dimensión política y la económica están inextricablemente unidas. Mientras más se intente eludir el problema del status de Puerto Rico más evidente se tornará la necesidad de enfrentarlo.

———

Mr. YOUNG. I thank the gentleman. Are you ready? Questions? I will recognize the Minority leader for questions.

Mr. SABLAN. I will yield to——

Mr. YOUNG. You have questions?

Mr. SABLAN. I will yield to Mrs. Torres.

Mr. YOUNG. Mrs. Torres, go ahead. You are getting closer. You keep it up, we will be hugging soon.

Mrs. TORRES. I know.

Mr. YOUNG. Oh, that sounds good.

Mrs. TORRES. Anything that gets me closer to you, Chairman, would be a wonderful thing. And thank you for allowing me to come before my colleagues.

My question would be to Mr. Miranda. Do you think that Puerto Rico's territory status is a cause of Puerto Rico's economic and fiscal problems, or just a contributing factor? Or do you think that the issues are totally distinct?

Mr. RODRÍGUEZ. First, let me qualify the concept of territorial status, that the present government does not accept as so. And "commonwealth" has been defined in other legal and constitutional relationships with the United States. But, nonetheless, I do not want to expand too much on that. The critical economic circumstances that we are facing in Puerto Rico are the consequence of many years of perhaps overspending. We have to admit that, in some cases, we should have been much more careful. But, nonetheless, in some way the island has been dealing with some difficulties in dealing with that sort of economic condition.

For instance, every state has a right to resort to a law that allows Chapter 9 to be implemented. Therefore, any municipality in any state can resort to it. Somebody has said that Puerto Rico wants to have a bail out. Puerto Rico is not interested in having a bail out by approving H.R. 870, and extending Chapter 9 to Puerto Rico.

Mrs. TORRES. I have one more question, so let me stop you there. My next question would be to Mr. Berríos. I want to make sure I get both of my questions on the record. We can follow up.

Puerto Ricans are leaving the island in huge numbers, and they are immigrating to the states. They are not necessarily leaving to other countries. In light of this, do you believe Puerto Rico's economy would perform better as a sovereign nation, or as a state?

Mr. BERRÍOS. It is Mr. Berríos.

Mrs. TORRES. Oh, Berríos.

Mr. BERRÍOS. Yes.

Mrs. TORRES. Disculpa.

Mr. BERRÍOS. No hay problema. Of course, I think the island economy will be much better off as a republic, because we would then have the tools necessary and the powers necessary to diversify our economy, to protect our production, to enter into commerce with other nations, to buy in cheaper markets. For a number of reasons—I could keep on enumerating them.

Now in Puerto Rico, we have been under depressive conditions since 2006. We have gone down 13 percent in our gross domestic product—13 percent. We have shrunk. And since 1970, we have been practically stagnated. This political status does not produce prosperity for the people of Puerto Rico, and we need the necessary tools to enter into the world market, keep up with the commerce with the United States, but have in our hands the means, as every other nation in the world does, including the United States, to promote its own economy. And the only way to do that is through the powers of independence.

Mrs. TORRES. As a sovereign nation?

Mr. BERRÍOS. As a sovereign nation, of course. I would pose the following rhetorical question to you—If independence is so bad, why do we have more than 200 and some-odd independent countries, including the United States, and only one territory?

Mrs. TORRES. Thank you, sir. I am not here to answer questions, I am here to ask them.

Mr. YOUNG. Thank you. Ms. Radewagen, you are up.

Mrs. RADEWAGEN. Thank you, Mr. Chairman.

I, too, want to welcome the panel of distinguished witnesses, the first panel.

I have a question for Congressman Pierluisi. Some pro-statehood advocates in Puerto Rico argue that Puerto Rico already voted for statehood in 2012, and should not have to vote again. You have pointed out the following: when Alaska and Hawaii were territories, they each held votes sponsored by the local government in which voters expressed a desire for statehood. Ultimately, Congress approved an Admission Act for Alaska in July 1958, and an Admission Act for Hawaii in March 1959. Those Acts of Congress provided for admission to occur once a majority of voters affirmed in a federally-sponsored vote that they desired statehood.

So you are essentially proposing the same procedure for Puerto Rico as was used in Alaska and Hawaii, right?

Mr. PIERLUISI. You are absolutely right, Madam Congresswoman. That is exactly what we are doing. We are following the path of Alaska and Hawaii. In both former territories, there were locally organized plebiscites—if I recall correctly, in Alaska, about 57 percent of the population supported statehood. And many years later, they finally got it. Alaska finally became a state.

But when Congress decided to legislate it, the admission of Alaska, it was conditioned upon a vote by the people of Alaska, basically ratifying the admission. And the vote happened, and to no surprise, then a much bigger majority of voters in Alaska supported the admission, and became a state.

The same happened in Hawaii. In Hawaii, if my recollection serves me right, the plebiscite result was about 67 percent or so. And years later, the same process happened. It was, coincidental, very close to the time when Alaska came in——

Mr. YOUNG. Would the gentleman cease for a moment? Whoever has that cell phone in this room, you better shut it off, or I will ask you to leave. It is impolite to have a cell phone on at any time.

You may proceed.

Mr. PIERLUISI. So, why am I proposing an up-or-down vote on the admission of Puerto Rico as a state? Simple. In 2012, a majority of the people of Puerto Rico, 54 percent, rejected the current status. And more people voted for statehood than any other option, including the current status. Given that scenario, the next logical step should be a vote on statehood. We had a yes or no in 2012, with respect to the current territory. Why not have one with respect to statehood? Anybody supporting statehood could vote yes.

My colleagues here, probably in all likelihood, would vote no, for whatever reasons. If you support independence for Puerto Rico, you would vote no. If you want Puerto Rico to be a sovereign nation with a compact of association with the United States, you could vote no.

So that is what I am proposing. It is fair. Nobody can say they would be excluded. All the voters in Puerto Rico could express themselves. And that is my position. Thank you.

Mrs. RADEWAGEN. Thank you, Mr. Chairman. I yield back.

Mr. YOUNG. My good lady friend from Guam.

Ms. BORDALLO. Thank you very much, Mr. Chairman, and I thank you for your leadership on addressing these issues that are so very important to the territories.

I welcome our former colleagues, the governors and the mayors and the other leaders from Puerto Rico. It is very nice to have you here with us in this very important hearing. I also commend Mr. Pierluisi, who has worked diligently to advance self-determination efforts, and who champions Puerto Rico's issues here in Congress.

Like our brothers and our sisters in Puerto Rico, the people of Guam aspire to determine our political future, and fully exercise our right to self-determination. I commend Puerto Rico's local leadership for their efforts to determine their political status, and I have urged local leaders on Guam to make similar efforts, so that we can move forward with our self-determination.

But this process is two-fold. Congress holds the institutional obligation to address the political status of Puerto Rico and the other territories under Article 4 of the Constitution. So I urge this committee to give due consideration to the views of the people of Puerto Rico on this issue.

My first question is to you, Mr. Pierluisi. You have argued that Puerto Rico's economic challenges make self-determination even more urgent now. You are an ardent advocate for statehood for Puerto Rico. If statehood vote were selected by the voters, and Congress approves it, how could statehood address Puerto Rico's difficult economic situation, which is the case now?

Mr. PIERLUISI. Well, the fact is that Puerto Rico has been lagging the states now for over four decades. Ever since the 1970s, Puerto Rico's unemployment, on average, has been 4 or 5 percent more than on the mainland. Ever since the 1970s, our growth has been lagging the one in the mainland. We have been behind. Income per capita, the GDP per capita in Puerto Rico, consistently has been about one-third the average in the states, and one-half the one for the poorest state, Mississippi.

So, it is pretty obvious to me—and let me add one thing, an additional fact which is very important. The debt that we are talking about, $72, $73 billion, it piled up under the current status. So it is pretty obvious to me that the common element here is that the current status is not working as a platform for Puerto Rico's economic development, for our quality of life.

To add insult to injury, our island is losing population like never before: 250,000 American citizens hopping on a plane and moving to the states to have the rights and the opportunities and the jobs they don't find in Puerto Rico. Actually, they are voting with their feet—because once they move to the states, they can vote for the President, they can elect Members of Congress, and they have equal rights in Federal programs, which we don't have in Puerto Rico.

Now, why would statehood be good for Puerto Rico? Well, let's talk about Hawaii and Alaska. In both Hawaii and Alaska you had growth, additional growth, once they became states. Let's talk about the fact that Puerto Rico's status, by its very nature, is not stable. It is insecure. There is political risk in Puerto Rico. So statehood is a permanent status. It is a stable status which will be very attractive, in terms of attracting additional investment to the island.

When we talk about Federal funding, because of the disparities we face, Puerto Rico would be receiving billions of additional funding that would flow into our economy if we become a state.

The bill I have introduced proposes basically a 4-year transition period, because the parity in Federal programs would happen gradually, as well as the taxes that would have to apply in Puerto Rico. You could phase them in, as well. So this wouldn't happen overnight, but I am sure that, once we put Puerto Rico on the path to statehood, we will grow, we will have a better quality of life, and our people will stay in Puerto Rico.

Ms. BORDALLO. Thank you very much. Mr. Chairman, I have another question. Are we going to make a second round?

Mr. YOUNG. I will let you ask it now.

Ms. BORDALLO. Good. Thank you, Mr. Chairman. This one is for Mr. Miranda.

Last year, Congress appropriated $2.5 million to Puerto Rico for a new plebiscite to resolve Puerto Rico's political status. Now I understand that the DOJ must approve the expenditure plan, ensuring that the plan is compatible with the Constitution and laws and policies of the United States. Has a plan been submitted? And would such a plan be compatible with the U.S. laws and policies?

Mr. RODRÍGUEZ. The plan seems compatible with the U.S. law, as you just said. My understanding is that there was a process for defining the status that we are going to be participating on a referendum. That definition had to be approved by the Secretary—by the Attorney General of the United States.

Where the due process stands now I really do not know, but I understand that at some point the Governor of Puerto Rico was getting involved in some conversations with the Department of Justice to address that point, and to have organized the process in Puerto Rico for that event to take place. I cannot assure you at this moment what is the actual state of that initiative that was very much welcome in Puerto Rico.

Ms. BORDALLO. Thank you very much for the information, and I yield back, Mr. Chair.

Mr. YOUNG. Do you want to ask questions? I recognize the Ranking Member.

Mr. SABLAN. Thank you very much, Mr. Chairman. And welcome again, everyone.

Now, this panel, let me get something straight. This panel consists of the heads of three political parties in Puerto Rico. Is that correct? Mr. Pierluisi is the President of the New Progressive Party; the Minister of Justice was the Popular Democratic Party; and Mr. Berríos is the President of Puerto Rico Independence Party? Is that correct?

Mr. RODRÍGUEZ. Yes, Mr. Chairman, but let me clarify. I am appearing here as a representative of the Governor in his executive functions. The Governor is also the President of the Popular Democratic Party in Puerto Rico, but I am not representing him on that particular position. So, therefore, I am not here representing the Popular Democratic Party. I am here appearing just as a representative of the Governor in his executive level.

Mr. SABLAN. So what, then, are you doing here, if you didn't get invited? We invited the President of the Popular Democratic Party.

Mr. RODRÍGUEZ. I understand that——

Mr. SABLAN. Why are you here?

Mr. RODRÍGUEZ. I am here because the Governor was invited in two different categories. He was invited as Governor, and he was invited as President of the Popular Democratic Party.

Mr. SABLAN. We made the invitation. We should know who we invited—and I think maybe you misunderstood, but we certainly don't misunderstand who we invited. Can I ask you a political question, then?

Mr. RODRÍGUEZ. You invited the Governor of Puerto Rico, and I am appearing here, representing the Governor of Puerto Rico in his capacity as governor, not in his capacity as president of the Popular Democratic Party.

Mr. SABLAN. I am confused now, because my questions are directed to you——

Mr. RODRÍGUEZ. You can direct the question to me, and I can decide if there is a——

Mr. SABLAN. You don't have to decide when to answer, sir. If you came here, I am assuming you came here as the head of a party. But you don't just come here—I mean this is by invitation only.

Mr. RODRÍGUEZ. I understand that.

Mr. SABLAN. So let me ask you—because the Governor was invited to testify. You agree with that, at least, right? About Puerto Rico's political status, and the connection between that party, the island's territorial status, and its economic problems—and let me ask you something, because—let me make it very clear. You want Chapter 9 for Puerto Rico, right? You think it benefits Puerto Rico——

Mr. RODRÍGUEZ. I view Chapter 9 of the bankruptcy law for Puerto Rico——

Mr. SABLAN. You agree with that, right?

Mr. RODRÍGUEZ. As the Attorney General, I assure you that that will be——

Mr. SABLAN. That Chapter 9 is allowed for states.

Mr. RODRÍGUEZ. Well——

Mr. SABLAN. States—the 50 states have the privilege of Chapter 9——

Mr. RODRÍGUEZ. Right. That is——

Mr. SABLAN. So you don't want to be a state, but you want what belongs to a state.

Mr. RODRÍGUEZ. Well, I will tell you.

Mr. SABLAN. All right.

Mr. RODRÍGUEZ. That could happen. Puerto Rico, as a commonwealth, can be treated differently from states. But, again, there are many other rights exercised by states that are also being granted to Puerto Rico. So why is there a difference regarding Chapter 9?

Mr. SABLAN. That is not just Puerto Rico——

Mr. RODRÍGUEZ. I do not understand that difference——

Mr. SABLAN. That is not exclusive to Puerto Rico, that is also to the other territories, including the Northern Marianas. But you want something that is a privilege extended to the 50 states, and you want that for Puerto Rico, but you don't want Puerto Rico to be a state.

You are holding on also—I understand your government——

Mr. RODRÍGUEZ. No, excuse me one second——

Mr. SABLAN [continuing]. You are holding on to $2.5 million that we appropriated for a plebiscite, a straight up or down question on whether Puerto Rico should favor statehood, Puerto Ricans favor statehood. You haven't had that plebiscite. We gave you the money, so it is no longer a question of money. So why don't you have that plebiscite?

Mr. RODRÍGUEZ. I explained, sir, that I am appearing here just——

Mr. SABLAN. Mr. Chairman, he is not going to answer my question. I yield back.

Mr. YOUNG. Thank you. Mr. Grijalva—I've got the Ranking Member and the Ranking Member. Which one is the rankest? He is the rankest?

Mr. GRIJALVA. We are both——

Mr. YOUNG. OK, you are both rankest? All right, Mr. Grijalva.

Mr. GRIJALVA. Thank you, Mr. Chairman. Very kind of you. And thank you for holding the hearing, and welcoming all the witnesses and former colleagues that are here with us today. And the sponsor of two pieces of legislation, our colleague on the committee, Mr. Pierluisi, who has worked long and hard in dealing with both the economic reality and challenges that are facing Puerto Rico now, as well as a piece of legislation that calls for a vote on the status and the statehood status—the Puerto Rico Statehood Admission Act, using the money that was appropriated previously, as the source for the election cost and the promotion of that.

The other one I think is very important, the submitted H.R. 870, because it is about equal treatment. And until the other issue, in terms of status and jurisdiction are settled, I think it is an important piece of legislation, because it talks about status. The 11 percent cut in Medicare only on the island, that is not an appropriate response to the economic crisis. Allowing Chapter 9 bankruptcy for state-owned—whether it be power or other authorities, and allowing the government-owned companies, as well as municipalities, to use Chapter 9, as would be the availability to any community or publicly-owned company here on the mainland.

So I want to thank the gentleman for that. I have a long, beautiful statement—10 pages—Mr. Chairman, that I will submit for the record.

Mr. YOUNG. I gladly have you submit it for the record.

Mr. GRIJALVA. Thank you.

[The prepared statement of Mr. Grijalva follows:]

PREPARED STATEMENT OF THE HON. RAÚL GRIJALVA, RANKING MEMBER, COMMITTEE ON NATURAL RESOURCES

Thank you, Mr. Chairman, and thank you for holding this hearing. I want to welcome all of the witnesses, particularly our former colleagues, Governors Fortuño, Acevedo Vilá and Romero. Today's hearing will look at the relationship between Puerto Rico's political status and the economic challenges they are facing.

The Island of Puerto Rico has been a territory of the United States since 1898. In all that time, the island's economy has seen its ups and downs. It became one of the great post-war economic success stories as a manufacturing powerhouse with a thriving middle class. But in the 1990s the Puerto Rican economy slowed with the repeal of the popular possession tax credit, which allowed U.S. corporations to defer paying U.S. income taxes on income earned in Puerto Rico. Since 2006, the economy has been in and out of recession. Today the unemployment rate is around 14 percent; 45 percent of the population lives below the Federal poverty line; and there's a fiscal crisis—a scramble to restructure debts of $73 billion. The Puerto Rico Electric Power Authority (PREPA) is said to be close to defaulting on approximately $8.6 billion in municipal bond debt.

Compounding the crisis is the fact that the territory has been losing population at a level not seen in decades. According to the *Washington Post*, "Puerto Rico lost 54,000 residents—1.5 percent of its population—between 2010 and 2012 alone. Since recession struck in 2006, the population has shrunk by more than 138,000 to 3.7 million, with the vast majority of the outflow headed to the mainland."

Additionally, because doctors practicing in Puerto Rico receive much smaller Medicare and Medicaid reimbursement rates than their counterparts on the U.S. mainland, the territory is facing a medical crisis. The Center for Medicaid and Medicare Services' (CMS) plans an 11 percent cut in Medicare Advantage reimbursements because of the rate formula. This has caused a steady drain of doctors on the island. This funding gap and exodus of trained professionals is expected to grow larger.

Representative Pierluisi believes that as long as Puerto Rico remains a territory—without equal treatment under Federal programs, forced to borrow heavily to make up the difference and without the ability to vote for the national leaders who regulate our economy—the island will not be in a position to overcome its economic problems. He has introduced H.R. 727, the Puerto Rico Statehood Admission Act, to address the question of the island's status.

He has also introduced a second bill, H.R. 870, to amend the U.S. Bankruptcy Code to enable Puerto Rico to authorize PREPA and other Puerto Rico government-owned corporations to adjust their debts under plans filed as debtors in Chapter 9 of the Bankruptcy Code. Governor Garcia Padilla and Congressman Pierluisi are in agreement that swift passage of H.R. 970 would go a long way in easing the pressure of default on PREPA and the other Puerto Rican government-owned corporations.

Mr. Chairman, I join the *New York Times* and other major publications in calling on Congress to pass H.R. 870 to allow Puerto Rican government-owned companies, as well as municipalities, to use Chapter 9.

Thank you again, Mr. Chairman. I yield back the balance of my time.

————

Mr. YOUNG. Are you through?

Mr. GRIJALVA. I am through and I yield back. Thank you.

Mr. YOUNG. Now Dr. Ruiz.

Dr. RUIZ. Thank you so much, Mr. Chairman. Mr. Chairman, our territories are a part of our Nation. Their residents are a part of our Nation. And, in fact, by an Act of Congress, they are American citizens. And yet, too often, our territories are left behind in major Federal legislation. The result of this inequality comes in the form of health disparities, severe income inequality, and in some cases, substandard living conditions.

For example, territory residents who have paid into the Medicare system do not have access to the same benefits they would be due as a state. The statistics on the disparities in Puerto Rico specifically are appalling. According to Puerto Rico's Medical Licensing and Studies Board, the number of physicians in Puerto Rico has dropped by 13 percent in the last 5 years, contributing to the severe primary health professional shortage in 34 medical underserved areas across Puerto Rico.

Compared to the states, Puerto Rico has less than half the per capita rate of emergency medicine physicians, which oftentimes serve as the individual's last safety net resource. And the reimbursement rate for physicians practicing on the island is said to go down even further, exacerbating these disparities. The people of Puerto Rico deserve to have access to the health care services that they have paid for, and deserve the opportunity to lead a healthy, full life. So I would like to ask you a question if we have enough time.

This question is for my colleague, Representative Pierluisi. How does Puerto Rico's territory status specifically harm the health and wellness of Puerto Rico's residents?

Mr. PIERLUISI. Thank you so much, Mr. Ruiz. And I will try to be brief and get to the point.

Actually, the situation we are facing is very similar when we talk about all the territories. The life of a territory is the life of American citizens in most—I understand that in American Samoa we are talking about nationals—unfortunately so. But we do not get equal treatment in Federal programs, including in Federal health programs. And that translates into worse quality of life for our people, particularly our vulnerable population.

What happens, for example, in the Medicaid program is that for years the U.S. Government was assuming roughly about 18 to 20 percent of the cost of Puerto Rico's Medicaid program, up to the Affordable Care Act. When the Affordable Care Act came about, I worked hard, as well as my fellow delegates from the territories, so that the Federal Government would enhance the funding we get. But we are still short at the moment, Puerto Rico basically—the U.S. Government is assuming 50 percent of the cost of our Medicaid program, but not resembling your Medicaid program.

In Puerto Rico, to give you an example, we afford health insurance to people up to roughly 80 percent of the U.S. poverty level. In the mainland, as you know, the Medicaid expansion is getting up to 134 percent of poverty level. So the Federal Government is not giving us, not even parity, equal treatment, for the population we have under the 100 percent of poverty level. To me, that is atrocious. It is unacceptable. These are American citizens, vulnerable American citizens, and the U.S. Government is not even funding——

Dr. RUIZ. So you have 1 minute. What is the solution?

Mr. PIERLUISI. The solution—I have a bill before this Congress proposing to fix all these disparities we have in Medicaid, Medicare, which you refer to, in a pragmatic, realistic way.

Let's say that just the Medicaid disparity is fixed. You are talking about roughly $1.2 billion that the government of Puerto Rico, is spending right now that the Federal Government would be spending. When we talk about fiscal issues in Puerto Rico, that, in and of itself, would solve the budget deficits that Puerto Rico has been dealing with, and would allow Puerto Rico to make the necessary contributions through its state pension system.

So, talk about the life of a territory. We are always lacking Federal funding, not to talk about lacking voting rights because, as I have said before, we don't vote for the President. Puerto Ricans have only me, a Resident Commissioner. I can debate, I can speak, but I cannot vote on the Floor—and I represent 3.5 million American citizens. That is not democratic, that is embarrassing.

So that is the situation. It definitely would help for you, for the Congress, to treat Puerto Rico fairly—at the very least, in Federal health programs.

Dr. RUIZ. Well, as a physician, I care very much in reducing those disparities, and ensuring that the citizens in Puerto Rico have the opportunity to live a life of wellness and a long, prosperous life, as well. Thank you.

Mr. YOUNG. Thank you, sir.

Mr. LaMalfa.

Mr. LAMALFA. I have no questions.

Mr. YOUNG. Commissioner, in your proposal with the new plebiscite—you say you have 5 years. On that plebiscite, what would happen if you had the plebiscite, and if the people of Puerto Rico voted for statehood that was automatic, then?

Mr. PIERLUISI. There are two pieces of legislation at issue. You have the appropriation that we approved, providing $2.5 million for a federally-sponsored plebiscite in Puerto Rico. The legislation speaks of having a vote to resolve the status issue, and it requires that the Attorney General of the United States basically bless whatever option is posed before the electorate. We don't want to waste time. We want to make sure that whatever the people vote on is something real, something possible.

Mr. YOUNG. What I am leading up to——

Mr. PIERLUISI. Yes.

Mr. YOUNG. The present legislation doesn't have—that is not finite. If they vote for it, there is another step. What if we were able to put something in the legislation so if they vote for it you become a state?

Mr. PIERLUISI. That is what H.R. 727 does. My bill, which has 108 co-sponsors—including me, 109—basically has a two-step process. You have an up-or-down vote on the admission of Puerto Rico as a state. And if a majority of the people support the admission, then it triggers the transition into the admission.

Mr. YOUNG. OK.

Mr. PIERLUISI. Depending on when the vote takes place, what the bill provides for is the admission of Puerto Rico, at the latest, in January 2021. We would be voting for President in the elections of November 2020, and we would be electing our Members of Congress in November 2020. Until then, Congress would be conforming the laws, Federal laws, so that Puerto Rico receives the same treatment states do.

Mr. YOUNG. This is a question for the total panel. And, like I said, I have been involved in this for a long time, because we were the leaders of the state recently, and then Hawaii, and then, of course, I hope Puerto Rico.

When we first got started in 1994, I warned at that time that status quo would not prevail and, in fact, you would be in economic problems. If we don't do something in the Congress, 20 years from now—I will start with you, Commissioner—where do you see Puerto Rico?

Mr. PIERLUISI. Quality of life is deteriorating incredibly fast. I see a bright future for Puerto Rico, because of the potential, the capacity of our people. But we cannot keep losing them. The current status is not providing them with the necessary quality of life, the necessary jobs and opportunities.

Congressman Ruiz was talking about doctors. By the way, the top surgeons in Texas, there are lots of Puerto Ricans there. And in Florida, they are all over. Not to talk about engineers, scientists. They are all over the states. The diaspora, we call. And we are losing them. Why are we losing them? Because they are American citizens, and the only thing they have to do to get a better quality of life is to hop on a plane and move to a state.

Mr. YOUNG. OK.

Mr. PIERLUISI. What are we aspiring to—to become a state.

Mr. YOUNG. The question was, if nothing occurs, you see a devastated island.

Mr. PIERLUISI. Yes.

Mr. YOUNG. OK.

Mr. PIERLUISI. Yes, the permanent solution to Puerto Rico's economic problems, social problems, is equal rights, is equality. All nations who have equal rights have prospered.

Mr. YOUNG. OK. I am just—the gentleman from the Governor's office?

Mr. RODRÍGUEZ. We see a brighter future for Puerto Rico. We are facing a very difficult financial situation. Actually, a crisis. Nonetheless, I understand that we have the capabilities to come across and bring the island to a brighter condition. We need the help that I mentioned before. We need to have an instrument to deal with the debt that we are carrying now. That is why we support extending bankruptcy Chapter 9 to Puerto Rico. That is a fact.

But besides that, I understand that all the capabilities are there. All the instruments are there in Puerto Rico. If we reorganize our debt and we can comply with our compromises, with holders of our debt, certainly Puerto Rico can come across and enter into a state of parity.

Mr. YOUNG. All right. Senator?

Mr. BERRÍOS. Well, the question is quite easy to answer with just the past products of the archives of the United States. The same downward spiral that started in 1970, and which has deepened to the present crisis since 2006, will continue. That will mean more dependence, more and more dependence, because Puerto Rico cannot exercise the potential of its productive capacity. And that will mean that the type of argument you have heard today for statehood, that is more and more and—billions of Federal funding as the Resident Commissioner said. Yet you will see more people aspiring for statehood for the wrong reasons.

Puerto Rico would then be on the verge of potentially becoming a ghetto state, and that is not the type of future I foresee for my land. We need the political powers, in order to develop our own economy and have a friendly relationship with the United States and with the rest of the world, not more and more dependency—more votes for statehood, because people believe statehood is just what the Resident Commissioner said, billions of dollars in funding.

Who aspires to that? We then have 80 percent living off food coupons or food checks, instead of 50 percent? That is the future of Puerto Rico if Congress doesn't act soon with more or less what I have proposed. Let's talk about this. Let's enter into the mutual collaboration process to find a way out for your benefit, and for our benefit.

Mr. YOUNG. I thank the panel. You have done well. I will tell you again, I personally don't believe—I have said all along, and don't get upset with me—if you are not going to be a state, you should become an independent nation. Either one. But the status quo is not working. We have watched this thing.

I said 21 years ago, I had the only vote on the House Floor on Puerto Rico—by one vote, by the way. I have watched the downward spiral. And these are great Americans, and to have this occur—I am just sitting here thinking, if something doesn't happen, if we don't do something, there is a possibility of revolution in

Puerto Rico, because you can't have a group of people that has American status and not have the rights that all other Americans have, and have a poverty level which is increasing.

This is a challenge to Congress. And the reason we are having these hearings is trying to get somebody to start talking about it, because this is a black eye on American soil. And we are going to continue to do that.

I want to thank the panel. You are excused.

Mr. BERRÍOS. Thank you very much.

Mr. YOUNG. Now we will call up the second panel. I have never seen so many fine, honorable governors in my life. I love it—the Honorable Luis Fortuño; the Honorable Carlos Romero, one of my dear friends, both of them were; the Honorable Acevedo Vilá; and the Honorable Carmen Yulin Cruz, who is a mayor; and Dr. Miriam Ramirez, former Puerto Rican State Senator.

And you all know the rules of the game. As soon as you all sit down and quit talking, we will start.

[Pause.]

Mr. YOUNG. Is everybody situated? You photographers get moving.

Because you are lined up this way, I am going to call on the Honorable Carlos Romero. Carlos, welcome. I can remember when I was in the Minority and you were in the Majority. You fought this battle then, as you are fighting it now. We may have different ideas, but I hope the people of Puerto Rico appreciated your dedication to a cause, and your word—crucially important.

So, you are up, you are first, you know the rules. I am pretty lenient, but you do what you have to do.

Mr. BARCELÓ. Thank you.

Mr. YOUNG. Turn that microphone on.

STATEMENT OF CARLOS ROMERO BARCELÓ, FORMER GOVERNOR OF PUERTO RICO 1977–1985 (PNP), SAN JUAN, PUERTO RICO

Mr. BARCELÓ. Mr. Chairman, members of the committee, good afternoon.

Mr. Chairman, I want to thank you on behalf of my fellow Puerto Rican Americans, who, as American citizens, demand equal rights and equal participation in the democratic process and the government of our Nation with our fellow citizens in the 50 states, for all your efforts and support to our long-time quest for equality.

Before we continue, I would like to ask you to ask yourselves these questions, and ask all the Members of Congress and the Senators to ask themselves these three questions: Do you believe in our Constitution and in our Nation's republican form of government? Do you believe, as our Constitution declares, that all men are created equal? And, do you believe that all U.S. citizens should have the right to vote and the right to representation at all levels of government?

If you answered yes to the third question, you should support and join our efforts to enact a bill for admission of Puerto Rico as a state.

I have dedicated 52 years of my adult life in a quest for equality for the people of Puerto Rico. We have been disenfranchised

American citizens for 98 years. We have been denied our right to participate in our Nation's democracy, and we have been denied any meaningful participation in our Nation's government. We have also been denied the same economic opportunities which have been available to our fellow citizens in the 50 states. We are, as a matter of fact, the world's last colony, with more than 1 million inhabitants. Under our Constitution, we are a U.S. territory. But in international, geopolitical terms, we are a colony.

In spite of the fact that we have been denied equality and participation in our Nation's democratic process ever since we were granted U.S. citizenship in 1917, more than 500,000 Puerto Rican Americans have served in our Nation's armed forces, and tens of thousands have shed their blood and lost life and limbs in defense of democracy, and in defense of our Nation. Puerto Rican Americans have more than earned their right to equal participation in our Nation's democratic process, as well as the right to vote for our President and to elect Senators and Representatives to Congress.

We are tired and increasingly upset to have to plead for equality. We are tired and increasingly upset to have to plead and beg for equal terms in Federal grants for education for our children. We are tired of pleading and begging for equal terms in Federal health care grants to provide health services to our medically indigent. We are tired of pleading and increasingly upset to have to beg for equal terms and Federal grants to help families with insufficient income to support their children. And we are tired and increasingly upset of being told that we don't qualify for Federal funding because we don't pay Federal income taxes.

How can Congress raise the issue of our non-payment of Federal income taxes when you know that we don't have the power to impose Federal income taxes on income earned in Puerto Rico? Only Congress has that power. And why doesn't Congress impose Federal income taxes on income earned in Puerto Rico? Because Congress knows that if they were to impose Federal income taxes on us without granting us equal voting rights and equal rights to elect Senators and Representatives to Congress, Congress would be invalidating our Nation's famous "No taxation without representation" battle cry to end the colonial relationship with Great Britain.

Yes, we are tired and increasingly upset by being denied the right to vote for our President, and the right to elect two Senators and Members of Congress that we would be entitled to as a state. And, we are particularly upset when we see our President and our Nation's Congress spending billions of dollars and sending our Nation's young men and women into harm's way, to bring democracy to countries such as Iraq and Afghanistan, where they don't understand it and don't want it. At the same time, they have kept and are still keeping 3.6 million U.S. citizens disenfranchised, discriminated against, and denied equality under the laws of the Nation for no less than 98 years.

It is no wonder that the United States is losing credibility and moral authority to preach democracy and to talk about strengthening democracy throughout the world. Our Nation is being ridiculed for its hypocrisy in spending billions of dollars and putting its young men and women in harm's way to bring democracy to people who don't want it or don't understand it, while at the same time they deny participation in the Nation's democratic process to 3.6 million American citizens because they live in Puerto Rico.

I have enclosed with my statement a disc containing some very insightful and satirical criticism of our Nation's hypocrisy with Puerto Rican Americans made by British comedian John Oliver. You will not only be enlightened by it, you will also enjoy it very much. And I also made a short editor—3 minutes and 30 seconds, that will be available also.

Yes, we must stop begging for equality and demand it loud and clear and belligerently, if need be. It is way past the time when Congress and the President should have put an end to our disenfranchisement and to our being denied equal opportunities under the laws of our Nation. How can anyone who claims to believe in democracy stand idly by without putting an end to the discrimination and the unacceptable inequality between the 3,600,600 American citizens who live in Puerto Rico and the 360 million fellow citizens in the 50 states?

Whether we demand equality or not, it is the Congress and the President's duty, as leaders of the world's greatest democracy, to put an end to this inequality and denial to participate in our Nation's democracy.

We have decided to ask for admission as a state. In November 2012, we held a referendum in Puerto Rico where the people were asked to vote whether they wanted to remain as a U.S. territory or not. Fifty-four percent of the voters said no, and 46 percent said yes. The referendum ballot had a second question to give the voters three options, to wit: statehood, sovereign commonwealth, or independence. A solid majority of 61 percent voted in favor of Puerto Rico being admitted as a state.

The solid majority vote for statehood in 2012 cannot be ignored. This Congress must address the issue and consider enacting a bill to provide for the admission of Puerto Rico as a state. The bill should establish the conditions and the process, as well as the fiscal and economic arrangements that must be implemented for Puerto Rico to be admitted as a state. The plebiscite, or referendum, to be held would allow the American citizens who reside in Puerto Rico the opportunity to accept or deny the offer. The ballot would be a simple yes-or-no vote. All those who oppose statehood could vote no, so they cannot complain that they were not offered an option to exercise the right to vote.

Of the 37 territories admitted to the Union since the 13 colonies joined to establish the United States of America, not a single one was disenfranchised for as long a period of time as we have been for 98 years. Not a single territory of the 37 admitted to the Union were deprived of equal economic opportunities and benefits for as long as we have. Not a single territory of the 37 territories who were admitted had as many citizens killed or wounded in the Nation's wars as we have had in the 98 years since we became American citizens.

The awareness of the importance and the benefits of being a state of the Union has become more obvious to Puerto Rican Americans as they suffer the effects of a worsening economic depression. As they increasingly feel they no longer have reasonable

33

opportunities to get a job or get ahead economically in the island, they are leaving Puerto Rico to look for substantially better opportunities in Florida, Texas, Georgia, New Jersey, New York, Connecticut, Pennsylvania, Massachusetts, Illinois, Ohio, and many other states. As a result, more and more Puerto Ricans realize that our island's economic future lies in becoming the 51st state.

We don't want our sons and daughters, our brothers and sisters, our grandchildren, our family and our friends to leave Puerto Rico. We want them to stay and enjoy the same opportunities available to our fellow citizens in the 50 states.

Puerto Ricans have also become more cognizant of the importance of having the right to vote for the President, and to elect Senators and Representatives to Congress in order to participate in our Nation's sovereignty. The value to our dignity, to our economic development, and to our self esteem in having two Senators and at least five Members of Congress is much more widely understood and sought after than ever before.

Rubén Berríos, the President of the Independence Party, claimed that we needed more political power. Definitely we need more political power, and definitely two Senators and five or six Congressmen have much more power than the President of Puerto Rico as an independent nation.

That, and much more is what millions of American citizens in Puerto Rico have been denied for 98 years. The time has come, not to beg or plead, but to demand equality. The time has come for Congress and the President to stop looking for excuses and enact a bill to admit Puerto Rico as a state, to be submitted to a vote in Puerto Rico.

Thank you, Mr. Chairman.

[The prepared statement of Mr. Barceló follows:]

PREPARED STATEMENT OF CARLOS ROMERO BARCELÓ, FORMER GOVERNOR OF PUERTO RICO

Mr. Chairman, members of the committee, good afternoon. Mr. Chairman I want to thank you, on behalf of all my fellow Puerto Rican Americans who, as American citizens, demand equal rights and equal participation in the democratic process and the government of our Nation with our fellow citizens in the 50 states of the Union, for all your efforts and support to our longtime quest for equality.

Before we continue, I would like you to ask yourselves the following questions:

1. Do you believe in our Constitution and in our Nation's republican form of government?
2. Do you believe as our Constitution declares, that, "all men are created equal", and
3. Do you believe that all U.S. citizens should have the right to vote for their President and to elect Senators and Representatives to Congress?

If you answered yes to the third question, you should support and join our efforts to enact a Bill for Admission of Puerto Rico as a state.

I have dedicated 52 years of my adult life in a quest for equality for the people of Puerto Rico. We have been disenfranchised American citizens for 98 years. We have been denied our right to participate in our Nation's democracy and we have been denied any meaningful participation in our Nation's government. We have also been denied the same economic opportunities which have been available to our fellow citizens in the 50 states. We are, as a matter of fact, the world's last colony with more than 1 million (1,000,000) inhabitants. Under our Constitution, we are a U.S. Territory, but in international geopolitical terms, we are a colony.

In spite of the fact that we have been denied equality and participation in our Nation's democratic process ever since we were granted U.S. citizenship in 1917, more than 500,000 Puerto Rican Americans have served in our Nation's armed forces and tens of thousands have shed their blood and lost life and limbs in defense of Democracy and defense of our Nation. Puerto Rican Americans have more than earned their right to equal participation in our Nation's democratic process, as well as their right to vote for our President and to elect Senators and Representatives to Congress.

We are tired and increasingly upset to have to plead for equality; we are tired and increasingly upset to have to plead and beg for equal terms in Federal grants for education of our children; we are tired of pleading and begging for equal terms in Federal health care grants to provide health services to our medically indigent; we are tired of pleading and increasingly upset to have to beg for equal terms in Federal grants to help families with insufficient income to support their children, and we are tired and increasingly upset at being told that we don't qualify for equal funding because we don't pay Federal income taxes.

How can Congress raise the issue of our non-payment of Federal income taxes when you know that we don't have the power to impose Federal income taxes on income earned in Puerto Rico. Only Congress has that power. And why hasn't Congress imposed Federal income taxes on income earned in Puerto Rico? Because Congress knows that if they were to impose Federal income taxes on us without granting us equal voting rights and equal rights to elect Senators and Representatives to Congress, Congress would be invalidating our Nation's famous "No taxation without representation" battle cry to end the colonial relationship with Great Britain.

Yes, we are tired and increasingly upset by being denied the right to vote for our President and the right to elect two Senators and the number of Members of Congress that we would be entitled to as a state. And, we are particularly upset when we see our President and our Nation's Congress spending billions of dollars and sending our Nation's young men and women into harm's way, to bring democracy to countries, such as Iraq and Afghanistan, where they don't understand it, nor want it. At the same time, they have kept, and are still keeping, 3.6 million U.S. citizens, disenfranchised, discriminated against and denied equality under the laws of the Nation for no less than 98 years.

It is no wonder that the United States is losing credibility and moral authority to preach democracy and to talk about strengthening democracy throughout the world. Our Nation is being ridiculed for its hypocrisy in spending billions of dollars and putting its young men and women in harm's way to bring democracy to people in Iraq and Afghanistan who do not understand it nor want it, while they deny participation in the Nation's democratic process to 3.6 million American citizens because they live in Puerto Rico. I have enclosed with my statement a disk containing some very insightful and satirical criticism of our Nation's hypocrisy with Puerto Rican Americans made by British Comedian John Oliver. You will not only be enlightened by it, you will also enjoy it.

Yes! We must stop begging for equality and demand it loud and clear; and belligerently, if need be. It is way past the time when Congress and the President should have put an end to our disenfranchisement and to our being denied equal opportunities under the laws of our Nation.

How can anyone who claims to believe in democracy stand idly by without putting an end to the discrimination and the unacceptable inequality between the 3.6 million American citizens who live their 360 million fellow citizens in the 50 states. Whether we demand equality or not, it is the Congress and President's duty, as leaders of the world's greatest democracy, to put an end to this inequality and denial to participate in our Nation's democracy.

We have decided to ask for admission as a state. On November 2012, we held a referendum in Puerto Rico where the people were asked to vote whether they wanted to remain as a U.S. Territory or not, and 54 percent of the voters said no and 46 percent said yes. The referendum ballot had a second question which gave the voters three (3) options, to wit: Statehood, Sovereign Commonwealth, or Independence. A solid majority of 61 percent voted in favor of Puerto Rico being admitted as a state.

The solid majority vote for statehood in 2012 cannot be ignored. This Congress must address the issue and consider enacting a bill to provide for the admission of Puerto Rico as a state. The Bill should establish the conditions and the process, as well as the fiscal and economic arrangements that must be implemented for Puerto Rico to be admitted as a state. The plebiscite or referendum to be held would allow the American citizens who reside in Puerto Rico the opportunity to accept or deny the offer. The ballot would be a simple Yes or No vote. All those who oppose statehood could vote No, so they cannot complain that they were not offered an option to exercise their right to vote.

Of the 37 territories admitted to the Union since the thirteen (13) colonies joined to establish the United States of America, not a single one was disenfranchised for as long a period of time as we have been for 98 years. Not a single territory of the 37 admitted to the Union were deprived of equal economic opportunities and benefits for as long as we have. Not a single territory of the 37 territories which were admitted had as many of its citizens killed or wounded in the Nation's wars as we have had in the 98 years since we became American citizens.

The awareness of the importance and of the benefits of being a state of the Union has become more obvious to Puerto Rican Americans as they suffer the effects of a worsening economic depression. As they increasingly feel they no longer have reasonable opportunities to get a job or get ahead economically in the island; they are leaving Puerto Rico to look for substantially better opportunities in Florida, Texas, Georgia, New Jersey, New York, Connecticut, Pennsylvania, Massachusetts, Illinois, Ohio and many other states. As a result, more and more Puerto Ricans realize that our island's economic future lies in our becoming the 51st state.

We don't want our sons and daughters, our brothers and sisters, our grandchildren, our family and our friends to leave Puerto Rico, we want them to stay and enjoy the same opportunities available to our fellow citizens in the 50 states.

Puerto Ricans have also become more cognizant of the importance of having the right to vote for the President and to elect Senators and Representatives to Congress in order to participate in our Nation's sovereignty. The value to our dignity, to our economic development and to our self-esteem having two (2) Senators and at (5) Members of Congress is much more widely understood and sought than ever before.

That, and much more is what millions of American citizens in Puerto Rico have been denied for 98 years. The time has come, not to beg or plead, but to demand equality! The time has come for Congress and the President to stop looking for excuses and enact a Bill to admit Puerto Rico as a state, to be submitted to a vote in Puerto Rico.

————

Mr. YOUNG. Thank you, Carlos. I have to say you said it very well—couldn't be said better. I did give you a little more time. I don't want the rest of you to get the idea I can be that lenient, but I might. Depends on how well you are doing. See, I was interested in what he had to say.

Mr. BARCELÓ. Thank you, Chairman. I know you have always been very supportive, and I remember the day in the House when we won by one vote.

Mr. YOUNG. Yes, right.

Luis, former Governor, former colleague. Welcome aboard.

STATEMENT OF LUIS G. FORTUÑO, FORMER GOVERNOR OF PUERTO RICO, 2009–2011 (PNP), WASHINGTON, DC

Mr. FORTUÑO. Thank you, Mr. Chairman. It is a pleasure to see you and so many other friends, and I thank you for your leadership on this issue.

The focus of today's hearing is on point, because the economic outlook of Puerto Rico is directly linked to the historical necessity of a permanent, constitutionally-defined political status. The current economic crisis is a cruel manifestation that territorial status is not a sustainable model for the political economy of America's last large and populous territory.

Real people are enduring harsh suffering because Puerto Rico's development is being suppressed by a century of even more severe constraints on growth than 32 other territories experienced before transitioning to a statehood economy. The dire situation that has developed under the commonwealth regime is demonstrated by graphs that I have provided to this subcommittee.

With the exception of a year and a half between 2011 and 2012, Puerto Rico's economy has been in negative territory during the last 9 years. The situation has turned critical during the last 30 months. We must reverse this accelerating decline and restore fiscal discipline, so that people can go back to work and families can recover optimism and prosperity.

But, Puerto Rico's full potential for economic success and job creation will not be realized until economic uncertainty generated by the island's unresolved political status is replaced by stability and full participation in the U.S. national economy. The 3.5 million U.S. citizens of Puerto Rico get it. That is why a 54 percent majority voted to end the current status in the plebiscite of 2012.

With voter turnout exceeding 78 percent, more than 61 percent of voters chose statehood over separate sovereign nation, with or without a treaty of free association. Results certified by the Puerto Rico Elections Commission confirmed that the total number of votes cast for statehood was greater than the total vote for the current status. That means the current status was defeated on the first ballot question, while statehood won a strong majority on the second ballot question.

There is no legal basis for assigning a meaning to blank ballots on the second question in the 2012 vote, while there is a historical precedent for a federally-sponsored vote to confirm the results of the 2012 plebiscite. That is why Congressman Pierluisi's bill, will empower voters either to confirm or reverse the 2012 vote for statehood.

H.R. 727 is fully consistent with the purpose of the 2014 bipartisan legislation in which Congress allocated $2.5 million for a new status vote. Its objective can be accomplished pursuant to the Pierluisi bill, under which the U.S. Attorney General still must certify the ballot question is legally valid under Federal law.

Yet, instead of open democratic self-determination, the ideological faction clinging to the status quo insists on obstructing the will of the people, as clearly expressed in the 2012 plebiscite. The defenders of the status quo can't even agree on a legally valid non-territorial status themselves.

The status proposals made in the past by the commonwealth party have not been constitutionally valid, and there is no indication that this time it will be any different. Meanwhile, as time passes, a steady and indeed unprecedented stream of U.S. citizens, denied both self-determination and equal economic opportunity in the territory, continue the exodus to acquire equal rights secured under our Constitution only through residence in a state.

But vast relocation within our national borders should not be required for U.S. citizens in a territory to attain equal rights. People know that in America equality includes government by consent, and in the United States that means voting rights in Federal elections secured only for residents of a state under our Constitution.

The real meaning of the 2012 vote is that decades of false doctrine on political status options have ended. A majority of your fellow citizens in Puerto Rico now understand that the most sacred fundamental rights of citizenship can be secured permanently and constitutionally only by citizenship in a state of the Union. This modern-day diaspora is a direct reflection of the inequities of the current territorial status and a direct response to the lack of action by Congress to address this flaw in our democratic way of life.

Every month, thousands of American citizens relocate from the island, leaving their homes and families behind, in search of equal opportunities, equal rights, and economic freedom that can only be attained in one of the 50 states. That is why supporters of statehood are not afraid to put the status we support to the test of an up-or-down vote. The most logical and democratic way for Congress to know where we stand as Americans is to allow us an up-or-down vote to confirm or overturn the 2012 results.

Thank you, and it is great seeing you again, Mr. Chairman.

[The prepared statement of Mr. Fortuño follows:]

PREPARED STATEMENT OF THE HON. LUIS G. FORTUÑO, FORMER GOVERNOR OF PUERTO RICO

Chairman Young, Ranking Member Ruiz and other members of this subcommittee: The focus of today's hearing is on point, because the economic outlook for Puerto Rico is directly linked to the historical necessity of a permanent, constitutionally defined political status.

The current economic crisis is a cruel manifestation that territorial status is not a sustainable model for the political economy of America's last large and populous territory. Real people are enduring harsh suffering because Puerto Rico's development is being suppressed by a century of even more severe constraints on growth than 32 other Federal territories experienced before transitioning to a statehood economy.

The dire situation that has devolved under the commonwealth regime is demonstrated by graphs from reports released by the Puerto Rico Government Development Bank that I have provided to this subcommittee (Exhibit A). With the exception of a year and a half between 2011 and 2012, Puerto Rico's economy has been in negative territory during the last 9 years. Said situation has turned critical during the last 30 months. We must reverse this accelerating decline and restore fiscal discipline so that people can go back to work and families can recover optimism and prosperity.

But there can no longer be any illusions about one transcendental truth. Puerto Rico's full potential for economic success and job creation will not be realized until economic uncertainty generated by the island's unresolved political status is replaced by stability and full participation in the U.S. national economy.

The 3.5 million U.S. citizens of Puerto Rico get it. That is why a 54 percent majority voted to end the current status in the plebiscite of 2012. With voter turnout exceeding 78 percent, more than 61 percent of voters chose statehood over separate sovereign nationhood, with or without a treaty of free association.

Results certified by the Puerto Rico Elections Commission confirm that the total number of votes cast for statehood (834,191) was greater than the total vote for the current status (828,077). That means the current status got an up or down vote and was defeated on the first ballot question, while statehood won a strong majority on the second ballot question.

There is no legal basis for assigning a meaning to blank ballots on the second question in the 2012 vote, while there is historical precedent for a federally-sponsored vote to confirm the results of the 2012 plebiscite. That is why Congressman Pierluisi's bill (H.R. 727) will empower voters either to confirm or reverse the 2012 vote for statehood.

H.R. 727 is fully consistent with the purpose of the 2014 bipartisan legislation in which Congress allocated $2.5 million for a new status vote. Its objective can be accomplished pursuant to the Pierluisi bill, under which the U.S. Attorney General still must certify the ballot question is legally valid under Federal law.

Yet, here we are in 2015, and instead of open democratic self-determination, the ideological faction clinging to the status quo insists on obstructing the will of the people as so clearly expressed in the 2012 plebiscite. The simple truth is that defenders of the status quo can't even agree on a legally valid non-territorial status definition. The status proposals made in the past by the commonwealth party have not been constitutionally valid, and there is no indication that this time it will be any different.

Meanwhile, as time passes, a steady and indeed unprecedented stream of U.S. citizens, denied both self-determination and equal economic opportunity in the territory, continue the exodus to acquire equal rights secured under our Constitution only through residence in a state.

But mass relocation within our national borders should not be required for U.S. citizens in a territory to attain equal rights. People know that in America equality includes government by consent, and in the United States that means voting rights in Federal elections secured only for residents of a state under Article I and Article II of the Constitution.

Thus, the real meaning of the 2012 vote is that decades of false doctrine on political status options have ended. A majority of your fellow citizens in Puerto Rico now understand that the most sacred fundamental rights of citizenship can be secured permanently and constitutionally only by citizenship in a state of the Union. This modern-day diaspora is a direct reflection of the inequities of the current territorial status and a direct response to the lack of action by Congress to address this flaw in our democratic way of life. Every month, thousands of American citizens relocate from the island, leaving their homes and families behind, in search of equal opportunities, equal rights and economic freedom that can only be attained in one of the 50 states of the Union.

That is why supporters of statehood are not afraid to put the status we support to the test in an up or down vote. As fate would have it, the most logical and democratic way for Congress to know where we stand as Americans is to allow an up or down vote to confirm or overturn the 2012 results.

*The opinions expressed in this testimony are my own and do not necessarily represent the opinions of Steptoe & Johnson, LLP, its employees or clients.

Attachment: Exhibit A

EXHIBIT A

In 2005 the EAI reached its highest level, and in 2006 it started to show significant year-over-year reductions.

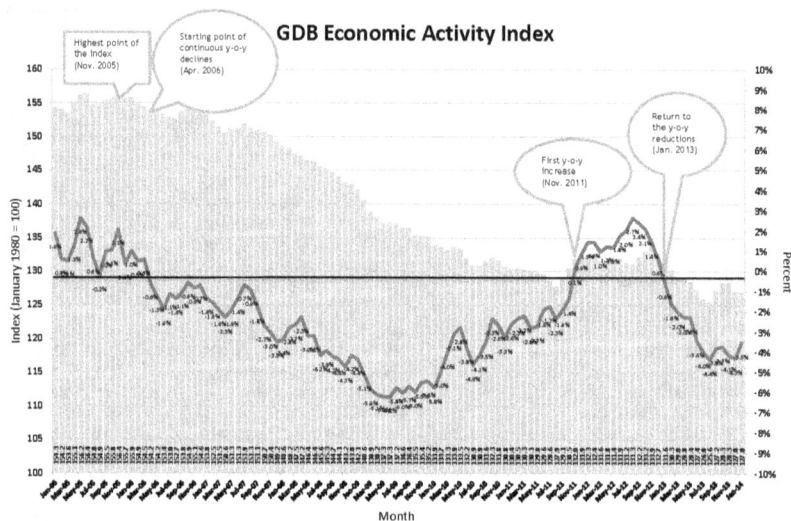

In January 2014, the GDB-EAI reflected a 3.5% y-o-y reduction, after showing a 4.3% y-o-y decrease in December 2013.

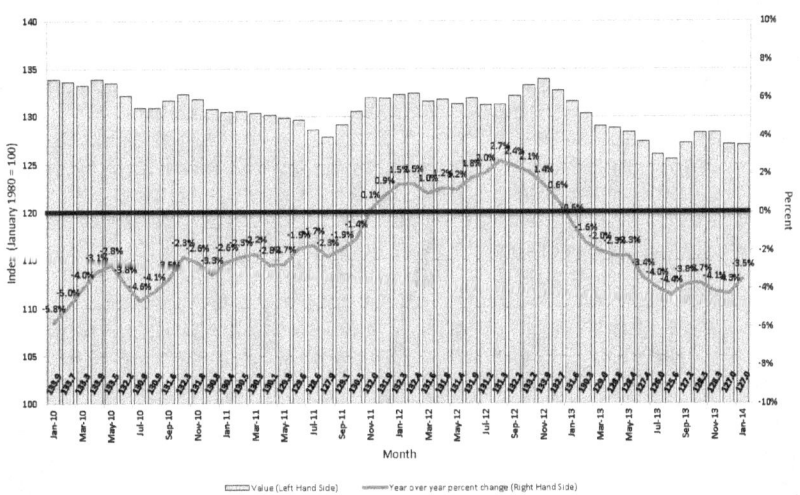

GDB Economic Activity Index

Changes to the new GDB-EAI (4)

...in terms of the year-over-year percent changes. The y-o-y percent changes remained similar to the previous estimates for the past three years.

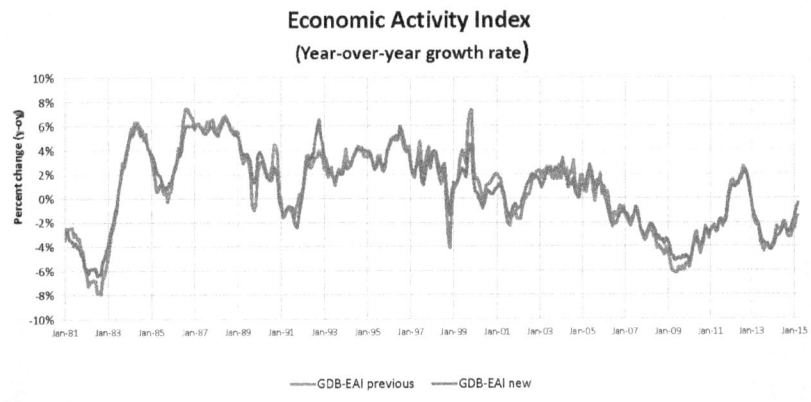

Economic Activity Index
(Year-over-year growth rate)

———

Mr. YOUNG. I thank you, Governor. And you are good at this. You learned something here. Five minutes, right on the button.

[Laughter.]

Mr. YOUNG. Acevedo Vilá, former Governor of Puerto Rico, former Commissioner, you are up.

STATEMENT OF ANÍBAL ACEVEDO VILÁ, FORMER GOVERNOR OF PUERTO RICO, 2005–2009 (PPD), SAN JUAN, PUERTO RICO

Mr. VILÁ. Thank you, Mr. Chairman. Thank you for the invitation.

I will start by saying the title of this hearing is quite revealing, since these procedures are not to analyze any pending legislation, and there is no prospect of legislative action in the near future.

On the other hand, the fact that this hearing combines the political relationship between Puerto Rico and the United States and the economic situation in the island is quite revealing, too. As far as I can remember, this is the first time any institution of any of the branches of the Federal Government have implicitly or explicitly recognized the important linkage between these two areas.

I have written and submitted a well thought-out document and a factually accurate testimony about the current economic crisis in Puerto Rico and what it means for our political status. I invite you to read it carefully. But since this committee has allowed me only 5 minutes to talk about such a critical point in time for our people, I am going to use my time today to request something of you, and make a plea for my people and my island. And I am sure that, from it, the subcommittee can draft a proper agenda of business to give adequate attention to our current economic situation.

While Puerto Rico first produced sugar and then soldiers, the United States told the world we were working together. While Puerto Rico provided thousands of our limited acres for military training and an open economy where American businesses flourish and prospered, you told the world we work together. We have gotten to where we are today together. Yes? A lot of the good and the bad were done by our own hands. But a lot of the good and the bad were done by your hands, too. Yes, it doesn't matter how you characterize it. The truth is that we have been in this together.

Now Puerto Rico is in a deep crisis that is threatening essential government services, including safety, education, and health care. Our economy has closed the door to hundreds of thousands of Puerto Ricans that have left their families and homes behind. But, contrary to the good old days, this time the U.S. Government is keeping distance. In this crisis, you say now we are not together.

I have no problem accepting our fault in the current crisis. But to pretend it is 100 percent our fault is incorrect and immoral. The economic crisis was worsened by the elimination by Congress of Section 936 of the Internal Revenue Code, and by fiscal policies and actions and lack of actions by the U.S. Government and of this Congress.

Our budget bubble happened at the same time that yours, under a monetary policy that fostered billions of dollars of unpayable debt. The Federal Reserve recognized its hand in the 2000 mortgage crisis, and set the money printing press to 'high' to solve it. But we have been left behind in the call.

Let me tell you, Congressmen and Congresswomen, in this crisis we are together. We worked together getting it, and work together in the consequences. Together, we will suffer the dislocations of uncontrollable migration. Together we will be hit by rising social programs and needs. Together we will face financial litigation by ravenous creditors looking for every penny, and with not even a law to organize the process.

No matter what you may think or want to believe, we are in this together. Actually, there is a Supreme Court case solved in 2007, which I quote in detail in my written testimony and it is included as an annex, that specifically addresses this issue in state—that in a situation where a U.S. territory faces economic insolvency, the U.S. Government is responsible and might be liable.

I have no doubt that we can solve our crisis and can come out of it stronger, if you realize that we are still together and come to the table to work with us. One-sided solutions won't work, whether they come from your side or ours.

I request of you a joint resolution of Congress, asking the Treasury Department and the Federal Reserve to roll up their sleeves and do more than just give advice. They need to get involved and be part of the solution. They have the power and the tools and the responsibility to do it. We are willing to sacrifice, but we need a fighting chance. No country, no state, no jurisdiction has gotten out of a crisis like ours without a bankruptcy law, a central bank intervention, or help from outside.

Call our relation a bilateral compact or a colonized territory. At this time it all means one thing: we are in this together. Thank you.

[The prepared statement of Mr. Vilá follows:]

PREPARED STATEMENT OF ANÍBAL ACEVEDO VILÁ, FORMER GOVERNOR OF PUERTO RICO

I want to thank this subcommittee and its Chairman for holding this hearing and for the invitation to testify. The first time I testified before the full Committee on Natural Resources was back in 1997 when I first became president of the Popular Democratic Party. A few years after that, I became a member of the House and of the committee and, as you know, later I was elected Governor of Puerto Rico. One thing is clear with the passing of all those years, there has been no action from Congress to deal with the status of Puerto Rico. And regarding the economic situation of the Island, the actions taken by Congress in the last 20 years have badly hurt our economy. It's clear we are in a worst situation today and that, yes, the United States has failed the people of Puerto Rico despite us being together for so long.

While Puerto Rico first produced sugar and then soldiers, the United States and our island worked together. While Puerto Rico provided thousands of our limited acres for military training and an open economy where American businesses flourished and prospered, you told the world we worked together. We have gotten to where we are today, together. A lot of the good and the bad were done by our own hands moreover a lot of the good and the bad were done by your hands, too. Now, Puerto Rico is in a deep crisis that is threatening essential government services, including safety, education and health care. But contrary to the good old times, this time the U.S. Government is keeping its distance.

I must say the title of this hearing is quite revealing. First, it is evident this hearing is not to analyze any pending legislation before this subcommittee, and therefore there's no prospect of actual legislative action in the near future. On the other hand, the fact that the hearing combines the issue of the political relationship between Puerto Rico and the United States and the economic situation in the island is quite revealing, too. As far as I can remember, this is the first time any institution of any of the branches of the Federal Government have implicitly or explicitly recognized the important linkage between these two areas.

For the last 2 years I have written and spoken about these two issues. I have submitted for the record a PDF file of a book I published in English in August of last year. I invite you to read it carefully, but I'll briefly explain my conclusions and commendations:

1. It is long past overdue a deep revision of the economic relationship between Puerto Rico and the United States. For many years this subcommittee and the full committee have approached the issue of that relationship from a

political perspective, but that has taken us nowhere other than to this major economic crisis in our modern history. The problems between Puerto Rico and the United States are economic as well as political.

2. After many decades of economic progress, the island is running out of time and the U.S. Government and its people need to know it's their problem too, because we are in this crossroads together.

3. The economy has been in recession for more that 8 consecutive years; government has been running deficits for more than 20 years and the government debt service of a debt surpassing $70 billion is unbearable. As I explain in more detail in my book, with the way things are moving, the day Puerto Rico will have to default in its payment of the debt is fast approaching and Puerto Ricans know that. A recent poll made public shows that 57 percent of the people are convinced "the debt, as it stands today, cannot be paid, the government should tell so to the bond holders, and a negotiation to restructure the debt should start."

4. This crisis is affecting the capability of the government of Puerto Rico to provide basic services to the people, including health.

5. If the government of Puerto Rico is not able to provide those services, it will become a problem for the U.S. Government. If Puerto Ricans continue leaving the island, that will become a U.S. problem. If Puerto Rico can't pay its debts, it will definitely become (and almost is) a U.S. problem. And as I will briefly explain here, the U.S. Government might even have a legal responsibility for that $70 billion debt.

Although Puerto Rico bears a great part of the blame for its economic crisis, the United States is also responsible for it. It's not only the elimination of Section 936 of the IRS Code in the 1990s without giving Puerto Rico another tool to compensate for that loss. It's also the indiscriminate application of Federal laws and regulations to our Island. The United States is the strongest and most developed economy of the world while Puerto Rico is still a developing economy. To impose the economic rules and standards of the most developed economy of the world upon a developing economy is a recipe for disaster.

The most recent report on Puerto Rico of the Federal Reserve Bank of New York (July 2014), specifically mentions as elements that hinder our economic growth, the application of the Federal minimum wage and the Jones Act to Puerto Rico, which are both clear examples of economic variables beyond our control. In fact, the Chairman of the Natural Resources Committee, Congressman Rob Bishop, has publicly expressed concerns about the negative economic impact the application of certain EPA rules can have in Puerto Rico due to our high costs of energy and the need we have to move toward more natural gas.

As someone said sometime ago, "it's the economy, stupid."

Regarding Puerto Rico's $72 billion public debt, there is also a shared responsibility. All that debt was originally incurred when Puerto Rico had a positive credit rating by the American credit agencies, and was all originally sold in the strongly regulated Federal municipal bond market. The years in which the amount of money being borrowed exploded, was during the time the Federal Reserve Bank carried out its expansive monetary policy with near zero interest rates. To that same extent, the crisis of the banking system in the United States, which almost collapsed in 2008, had a similar origin. In our case, if we were incurring in too much debt, it was in part because the Feds kept the interest rates artificially low, which in turn opened the appetite in Wall Street for higher yielding bonds from Puerto Rico, all under the watchful eyes of the various Federal credit rating agencies.

I firmly believe the United States has to be part of the solution to Puerto Rico's economic and debt crises. I firmly believe we are in this together, and not as a legal argument, but because there is a shared responsibility. But at the end of the day, it might be the legal responsibility that will move the United States to action. The U.S. Supreme Court might decide that the U.S. Government is responsible for Puerto Rico's debt.

Let's understand how that debt was incurred. Puerto Rican bonds are regulated by Federal law (Section 745 of title 48 of the United States Code). Our bonds have been marketed based on a Federal law, playing by the Federal rules. This provision was adopted in 1917 as part of the plenary powers of Congress over the territory of Puerto Rico. Congress ordered the other states not to tax our bonds, something that clearly Congress has no power to do with regards to specific state bonds.

For the last 25 years or more, the official position of the U.S. Department of Justice, the House and Senate committees with jurisdiction over Puerto Rico and the White House reports of both presidents, George W. Bush and Barack Obama, have established that even after the establishment of the Commonwealth of Puerto Rico in 1952, Puerto Rico is still a non-incorporated territory. The most recent report from the White House specifically states: "under Commonwealth option, Puerto Rico would remain, *as it is today*, subject to the Territory Clause of the U.S. Constitution" (March 2011). Therefore, it could be argued the powers that Congress had to establish Section 745 in 1917 granting triple tax exemption to our bonds, are the same powers they have today to keep that exemption and impose it upon the 50 states. All this legal and financial history is a clear indication the U.S. Government has a shared responsibility over our debt.

In January 8, 2007, the U.S. Supreme Court ruled on the case of *Limtiaco* v. *Camacho* (549 U.S. 483 (2007)). The issues are quite particular, but the rationale of the decision is very interesting. There was a "local" dispute between the Governor of Guam and his attorney general regarding a bond issuance and whether it was an infringement of a debt limitation disposition included in the Federal Organic Act of Guam. The Governor obtained a declaration from the Guam Supreme Court that the issuance of bonds to fund the territory's continuing obligations, authorized by Guam's legislature, was not in violation of debt limitation disposition contained in the Organic Act of Guam, contrary to the contention of Guam's attorney general. The U.S. Court of Appeals for the Ninth Circuit dismissed the attorney general's appeal. The U.S. Supreme Court reversed. It is the last paragraph of the Court's opinion, written by Justice Thomas, that brings some light to the Federal Government's responsibility in regards to the debt of a territory:

> "It may be true that we accord deference to territorial courts over matters of purely local concern. This case does not fit that model, however. The debt-limitation provision protects both Guamanians and the United States from the potential consequences of territorial insolvency. Thus, this case is not a matter of purely local concern."

For many years during my political life I have argued against the definition of Commonwealth as a territory. That was my main argument when I first testified before this committee back in 1997. Nevertheless, the official position of this committee and the U.S. Government is that we are still a territory. If that is the case, taken together with cited Section 745, there is a strong argument the United States might bear "the potential consequences" of Puerto Rico's insolvency and that the $72 billion debt "is not a matter of purely local concern." The Federal Government cannot say that we "remain, *as it is today*, subject to the Territory Clause of the U.S. Constitution" in order to deny Puerto Rico the powers to solve our economic and social crisis, and now turn around and say they have no responsibility regarding our debt because the debt crisis is a "a matter of purely local concern."

You cannot have your cake and eat it too.

THE CLOCK IS TICKING. The government of Puerto Rico has entertained many important economic, fiscal and government reform initiatives. They were urgent and needed, but the crisis is beyond all that. If the U.S. Government and its people do not realize soon Puerto Rico is a problem that needs to be addressed with new thinking and new approach, the United States will soon wake up with a new domestic crisis with international ramifications.

I have no doubt that we can solve our crisis and come out of it stronger if you realize that we are still together and come to the table to work with us. One-sided solutions won't work whether they come from your side or ours.

That's why I request a joint resolution of Congress requesting the Treasury Department and the Federal Reserve to roll up their sleeves and do more than just give us advice. They need to get involved and be part of the solution. They have the power and the tools to help us. We are willing to sacrifice, but we need a fighting chance. No country, no state, no jurisdiction has gotten out of a crisis like ours without a bankruptcy law, a central bank intervention or help from outside.

Call our relation a bilateral compact or a colonized territory. At this time, it all means one thing: we are in this together.

Thank you for inviting me and don't hesitate to contact me if you want a deeper discussion.

––––––––

Mr. YOUNG. Thank you, Governor.

Carmen, the Mayor of San Juan. Beautiful town, great people. Haven't had the privilege of meeting you yet. Thank you. You are welcome.

STATEMENT OF CARMEN YULIN CRUZ SOTO, MAYOR OF SAN JUAN, 2013–PRESENT (PPD), SAN JUAN, PUERTO RICO

Ms. SOTO. Thank you very much, Chairman and members of the committee, for the opportunity. Puerto Rico has enjoyed, in the past, a commonwealth status responsible for catapulting our economic development. But the world has changed. That which once made us successful now lacks the necessary tools to handle today's reality. Ultimately, any viable political status must provide the necessary economic tools to engage and sustain an equitable economic growth while strengthening our democracy.

Puerto Rico has been denied these tools far too long, and as long as our options are defined by the powers of this Congress, we will always be at your mercy. The measure of our success will always be limited by the vastness of your control over our affairs.

I admit, as did the Governor, that our current financial situation has a healthy dose of shared responsibility. For years, we engaged in chronic patterns of unhealthy indebtedness, while you denied us or took away the few tools we have at our disposal. Sir Winston Churchill once said, "Give us the tools to win this war." It is profoundly evident that our political status will determine the tools we have at our disposal to wage and win the economic war we are immersed in.

Far too long you have benefited from our inability to reach a consensus in the status question. No more—you can no longer use that as an excuse to neglect your responsibility. Paraphrasing Gandhi—"The time has come for you to recognize that you are masters in somebody else's land." The time has come for you to put in motion a true self-determination process which ensures all voices and all options have equal access to the formulation and implementation of the status resolution issue.

I come before you as one of the 454,768 Puerto Ricans who, in November 2012, voted to transform the present commonwealth relationship into a non-territorial, non-colonial, free associated state, to request that Congress include said option in any status-defining process in a manner which is distinguishable from other status options.

Said new status is based on the recognition of the sovereignty of the people of Puerto Rico and our inalienable right to choose whichever form of government we see fit. The ELA Soberano will be forged on a compact of association in accordance with international law. We aspire, as the majority of Puerto Ricans, to guarantee for present and future generations the common bond of U.S. citizenship.

Of course, any serious self-determination process—and I must clarify I am personally in favor of a status assembly—will take time. However, there are matters which may be addressed immediately.

One, we must ensure Resident Commissioner Pedro Pierluisi's bill to include Puerto Rico in Chapter 9 of the U.S. bankruptcy law is swiftly approved, so that we have the legal capability to restructure our obligations and pay them in a manner consistent with the well-being of our people. We recently tried to deal with this issue and the Federal court ruled against us. I fully support this bill.

Two, give us the authority to enter into commercial agreements with other countries, as well as partially or fully exempt us, just as the Virgin Islands next to us, from the yoke placed upon us by the Jones Act.

You have the power to help Puerto Rico. Now you must exercise it. You have the moral obligation to end the trite pilgrimage of Puerto Ricans looking for the status question to be resolved. You must move forward. I assure you, you will be met by an alliance of relentless people who know how—who have in the past and will in the future, once again, overcome adversity. Thank you very much, Mr. Chairman.

[The prepared statement of Ms. Soto follows:]

PREPARED STATEMENT OF CARMEN YULIN CRUZ SOTO, MAYOR OF SAN JUAN, PUERTO RICO

I want to thank the Chairman and members of this subcommittee for today's invitation to share my views regarding Puerto Rico's political status and economic outlook. My name is Carmen Yulin Cruz Soto and I currently serve as Mayor of San Juan, Puerto Rico.

Puerto Rico has enjoyed a Commonwealth status responsible for catapulting our economic development. But the world has changed; that which once made us successful now lacks the necessary tools to handle today's reality. Ultimately, any viable political status must provide the necessary economic tools to engage in sustained and equitable economic growth while strengthening our democracy.

Puerto Rico has been denied these tools far too long and as long as our options are defined by the powers of this Congress, we will always be at your mercy. The measure of our success will always be limited by the vastness of your control over our affairs.

I admit, our current financial situation has a healthy dose of shared responsibility. For years, we engaged in chronic patterns of unhealthy indebtness, while you deny us—or have taken away—the few tools we have at our disposal. Sir Winston Churchill once said: "Give us the tools to win this war." Have no doubt we are in the midst of an economic war. It is profoundly evident that our political status will determine the tools we have at our disposal to wage and win that war.

Far too long you have benefited from our inability to reach a consensus in the status question. No more: you can no longer use that as an excuse to neglect your responsibility. Paraphrasing Gandhi: "the time has come for you to recognize that you are masters in somebody else's land." The time has come for you to put in motion a true self-determination process which ensures all voices and all options have equal access to the formulation and implementation of the status resolution issue.

I come before you as one of the 454,768 Puerto Ricans who on November 2012 voted to transform the present Commonwealth relationship into a non-territorial, non-colonial Free Associated State to request that Congress includes said option in any status defining process in a manner that is distinguishable from the present territorial Commonwealth, as well as from statehood and independence.

Said new status is based on the recognition of the sovereignty of the people of Puerto Rico and our inalienable right to choose whichever form of government we see fit.

The ELA SOBERANO will be forged on a compact of association in accordance with International Law. The definition presented to voters on 2012 stated that "(s)uch agreement would provide the scope of the jurisdictional powers that the People of Puerto Rico agree to confer to the United States and retain all other jurisdictional powers and authorities." We aspire, as the majority of Puerto Ricans, to guarantee, for present and future generations, the common bond of U.S. citizenship.

Any serious self-determination process will take time; however there are matters which may be addressed immediately:

1. Ensure Resident Commissioner Pedro Pierluisi's bill to include Puerto Rico in Chapter 9 of the U.S. Bankruptcy Law is swiftly approved so that we have the legal capability to restructure our obligations and pay them in a manner consistent with the well-being of our people. We recently tried to deal with this issue and the Federal Court ruled against us. I fully support this bill.

2. Give us the authority to enter into commercial agreements with other countries as well as partially or fully exempt us from the yoke placed upon us by the Jones Act.

You have the power to help Puerto Rico now; exercise it! You have the moral obligation to end the trite pilgrimage of Puerto Ricans looking for the status question to be resolved; move forward.

I assure you, you will be met by an alliance of relentless people who know how and will in the future once again to overcome adversity.

Thank you.

————

Mr. YOUNG. I thank the good mayor. Now we have Miriam Ramirez, M.D., former Puerto Rican State Senator.

STATEMENT OF MIRIAM J. RAMIREZ, M.D., FORMER PUERTO RICO STATE SENATOR, 2001–2004 (PNP), FOUNDER, PUERTO RICANS IN CIVIC ACTION, ORLANDO, FLORIDA

Ms. RAMIREZ. Yes, Mr. Chairman. It has been a privilege to know you and count on your solid and courageous support to advance our struggle to achieve equal rights for the almost 4 million disenfranchised citizens in Puerto Rico.

Decades ago you responded with your full support when more than 350,000 Puerto Ricans petitioned Congress for statehood. Today, you are again giving us an opportunity to obtain our equal rights and obligations as U.S. citizens of this great Nation.

In my testimony here in Washington, on May 22, 1986, Congressman Morris Udall was the Chairman. And I mentioned our full rights as citizens being the fundamental reason for the poor economic performance of Puerto Rico. Today I want to focus my testimony on the negative consequences of the Federal tax regime that has kept Puerto Rico labeled as a foreign jurisdiction for almost a century.

I have been hearing people here talking about the dire life in Puerto Rico, how bad it is. But did you know it is only for a group of people? Because we have a big percentage of people in Puerto Rico who relocate from the United States, and can live in Puerto Rico tax-free from Puerto Rico and for the Federal Government. I hate to get away from my testimony. I will continue reading it, but I am just too passionate about this issue.

In 1996, I have been hearing here about how, after Section 936 was eliminated, the former Section 936 firms used Puerto Rico's foreign tax status and converted to controlled foreign corporations (CFCs)—corporate welfare. However, the CFCs in Puerto Rico are not obligated to create local jobs or to generate any real investment in order to benefit from the Federal tax deferral. Using transfer pricing abuses, the CFCs in the island are causing the U.S. Treasury to lose billions in Federal tax revenue without creating jobs and investment in the island.

The Senate Permanent Subcommittee on Investigations identified one company in Puerto Rico—just one—that has come public that benefits from a tax saving of $22 million a year per employee, and they have about 170 employees. And most of them—I don't have the statistics—are on part-time jobs. The U.S. taxpayer is also maybe paying for some of this money that is coming and creating this dependence in Puerto Rico.

Also, to exploit the special Federal tax code of Section 933, the pro-statehood administration adopted—the former one—two laws in 2012, Act 20 and Act 22, to entice millionaires who reside in the 50 states to relocate to Puerto Rico by taxing their corporate profits from exported services at a flat 4 percent rate, and allowing those profits to be paid out to these owners free of Puerto Rico income tax. Bring them here and ask them how they feel living in Puerto Rico is.

Thus, the CFC regime in Puerto Rico has become a significant drain of tax revenue, and a formidable opponent of statehood for Puerto Rico. Keeping Puerto Rico as a foreign country, as we are coded in the IRS, inside the United States, undermines the U.S. Federal tax base, and creates unfair competition against local communities in the 50 states and in Puerto Rico. But the truth is that Puerto Rico is governed by the CFC regime and the economic power of the super-billionaires who relocate without paying taxes.

But that is not the only damage they do. They have the most powerful public relations army in the world, ready to lobby and fight against anything that endangers this outrageous tax evasion scam. The worst concern for them is that Puerto Rico becomes a state of the Union, so they throw their lobbyists out here. And you will have, enclosed in my written testimony, a letter from one of the lobbyists, precisely after the plebiscite, demeaning the results of them.

This is the reason that I find it impossible to fight against the CFCs if we want to achieve statehood. We have to make the CFCs part of the political status solution. Mr. Chairman, I propose that a statehood bill, with the defining terms of admission, and a 20-year transition period for maintaining the CFCs in Puerto Rico, come out of your committee.

There is a precedent for previous statehood bills to include temporary tax benefits, and a transition period was included in Senate Bill 712 of 1990.

Please do not hold any more plebiscites with the various options, we have been there and done that. We now put the ball in your side of the court. Define the admission terms and ask our people.

And, Mr. Sablan, we are paying for Mr. César Miranda's testimony, even though he is reporting for the Governor. He is reporting for one of the status options, so we are basically paying for that.

[The prepared statement of Ms. Ramirez follows:]

PREPARED STATEMENT OF MIRIAM J. RAMIREZ, MD, FORMER PUERTO RICO STATE SENATOR

Honorable Chairman Young and members of the committee: My name is Miriam Ramirez, I am a medical doctor, former Senator of the New Progressive Party in Puerto Rico, and founder of a non-partisan grassroots movement, called Puerto Ricans in Civic Action, which gathered more than 350,000 individually signed petitions for statehood and delivered them to Congress in the 1980s.

Mr. Chairman, it is has been a privilege to know you and count on your solid and courageous support to advance our struggle to achieve equal rights for the almost 4 million disenfranchised U.S. citizens in Puerto Rico. Decades ago you responded with your full support when more than 350,000 Puerto Ricans petitioned Congress for statehood. Today you are again giving us an opportunity to obtain our equal rights and obligations as U.S. citizens of this great Nation.

In my testimony to this committee on May 22, 1986, when Congressman Morris Udall was the chairman, the focus of the hearing was the lack of economic growth and welfare dependency in Puerto Rico. Back then I identified our lack of full rights as U.S. citizens as the fundamental reason for the poor economic performance of Puerto Rico, compared to other states. Today I want to focus my testimony on the negative consequences of the Federal tax regime that has kept Puerto Rico labeled as a "foreign" jurisdiction for almost 100 years.

There are two Federal tax acts which have defined Puerto Rico's tax identity since it became a U.S. territory in 1898. The first law—the Revenue Act of 1921—classified Puerto Rico as a "foreign country" for tax purposes. The second law, enacted by Congress in 1996, eliminated Section 936 of the tax code, which was used then to promote new manufacturing jobs and investments in Puerto Rico.

What happened in Puerto Rico after 1996? The former Section 936 firms used Puerto Rico's "foreign" tax status to obtain the benefits of tax deferral, converting to Controlled Foreign Corporations (CFCs). Unlike the former Section 936 program, however, the CFCs in Puerto Rico do not have to create jobs and generate real investments to benefit from Federal tax deferral. Worse, the U.S. Treasury does not produce reports that inform Congress whether the CFCs create jobs and real investment in Puerto Rico. Today we know they don't.

The CFC regime in Puerto Rico has become a significant drain of tax revenue and a formidable opponent of statehood for Puerto Rico. Using transfer pricing abuses, the CFCs in the Island are causing the U.S. Treasury to lose billions in Federal tax revenue without creating jobs and investment in the Island. One company in Puerto Rico was identified by the Senate's Permanent Subcommittee on Investigations with tax savings of $22 million per employee, and only generated 177 employees. Other details of this tax abuse are presented in the Appendix.

Keeping Puerto Rico as a "foreign" country inside the United States undermines the U.S. Federal tax base and creates unfair competition against local communities in the 50 states. For example, in 2010 the Puerto Rico government imposed a 4 percent excise tax on CFCs in Puerto Rico in order to pay for a significant reduction in income taxes at the local level. Normally, excise taxes cannot be used as foreign tax credits that reduce the U.S. tax liability dollar for dollar. However, in the case of the Puerto Rico's 4 percent excise tax on the U.S. CFCs, the IRS took the position that it would not challenge if U.S. corporations claim a U.S. foreign tax credit. In contrast, taxes imposed in the 50 states can be deducted when calculating Federal income tax, provided they are attributable to the conduct of the corporation's business. Effectively, the U.S. Treasury subsidized Puerto Rico's 4 percent excise tax increase almost dollar for dollar. This unrecorded tax expenditure is not available in the 50 states.

Politically, the CFCs are effectively in control of our major political parties and their governing agenda. Whenever the people put pressure for a process of self determination, millions of dollars appear out of nowhere to campaign against statehood, since it will be the death knoll for the CFC scam.

There are hundreds of CFCs in Puerto Rico that make enormous campaign donations to the political leaders in Puerto Rico, many of whom are here today in this hearing. I have concluded it is impossible to fight the CFCs if we want to achieve statehood in Puerto Rico. We have to make the CFCs part of the political status solution.

Mr. Chairman, I propose that the statehood bill for Puerto Rico that comes out of your committee include a 20-year transition for maintaining the CFCs in Puerto Rico. There is a precedent for adding temporary tax benefits in statehood bills and a transition period was included in the Senate Bill 712 in 1990.

There is another tax provision that goes back almost 100 years that is keeping Puerto Rico back, preventing us from receiving the full benefits of U.S. citizenship, namely Section 933 of the Internal Revenue Code (IRC).

As you know, Mr. Chairman, Congress in 1917 granted U.S. citizenship to individuals born in Puerto Rico. Thus, a person born in Puerto Rico is subject to the U.S. tax laws. However, Section 933 of the IRC exempts from U.S. taxation the Puerto Rico-source income obtained by bona fide residents of Puerto Rico.

To exploit this special Federal tax status, the "pro-statehood" administration of former Governor Fortuño adopted two laws in 2012. Act 20 entices millionaires who reside in the 50 states to locate to Puerto Rico by taxing their corporate profits from exported services at a flat 4 percent rate and allowing those profits to be paid out to the owners free of Puerto Rico income tax.

Act 22 grants new Puerto Rico residents a 0 percent rate on locally sourced interest and dividends as well as all capital gains accrued after they become residents, in order to attract hedge fund managers and active traders. So far 509 tax refugees have been granted Act 22 status and another 600 will get it this year, according to the Puerto Rico's Department of Economic Development & Commerce.

This egregious legislation is effectively eroding the Federal and state income tax base and converting Puerto Rico into a tax haven in the U.S. backyard. We are despised by the Members of the U.S. Congress of New York, California, Connecticut and other states where these millionaires used to live. This is what our political leaders, of both major parties, have turned Puerto Rico into—a tax haven in the U.S. backyard for a few hundred millionaires.

Mr. Chairman, the citizens of Puerto Rico are outraged by these shameful tax benefits given to a few hundred millionaires, while the rest of us have been subject to multiple tax increases by the present Administration in the last 3 years. We ask Congress to end this tax abuse, and eliminate Section 933 of the Internal Revenue Code immediately.

Some observers in the past have expressed the opinion that the residents of Puerto Rico are better off because Federal income tax laws do not apply in the Island. This opinion is not correct for two reasons:

1. The Federal income tax provides job incentives that are lacking in Federal direct spending programs. For example, the exclusion of Puerto Rico residents from the Federal income tax has prevented almost 60 percent of working families from receiving the Federal Earned Income Tax Credit (EITCs). The Federal income tax could be used as an effective tool to increase Puerto Rico's 40 percent labor force participation rate, which is the lowest in the United States.[1]

2. The introduction of the Federal income tax, with the administrative support of the Internal Revenue Service, would increase the effectiveness of the local tax administration in Puerto Rico. Local tax auditors in the Department of Hacienda have experienced a 50 percent decrease in the last 6 years, at the time when the underground economy in Puerto Rico has grown to about 25 percent of the market economy.

Previous congressional studies have already shown the benefits of participating in the Federal tax system. For example, GAO in 1996 found that if IRC tax rules are applied to residents of Puerto Rico, the average EITC earned by eligible taxpayers would be $1,494, taxpayers would owe around $623 million in Federal income tax before taking into account the earned income tax credit (EITC), and the aggregate amount of EITC would total $574 million. About 59 percent of the population filing individual income tax returns would earn some EITC, and 41 percent of the households filing income tax returns would have positive Federal income tax liabilities, greater than the EITC received. Thus, the introduction of the Federal income tax in Puerto Rico for individuals would generate a wealth transfer from higher-income individuals who would pay Federal income taxes, to lower-income earners who would receive a refundable credit.[2]

Mr. Chairman, this is the right moment to draft legislation to resolve the political status of Puerto Rico, and include Puerto Rico in the U.S. tax code, with all the responsibilities and privileges of U.S. citizens. This historic change can be achieved by *deleting* Section 933 of the Internal Revenue Code, and *defining* corporations incorporated in Puerto Rico as U.S. Corporations, for tax and other purposes.

With Puerto Rico's full inclusion in the tax code, Congress can stop transfer pricing abuses and create effective tax benefits that generate real jobs and promotes tangible investments in Puerto Rico through specific legislation that treat U.S. citizens in the Island in a manner similar to other communities in the 50 states. There is a real opportunity to draft effective legislation for Puerto Rico that creates a direct link between each dollar of Federal tax benefits to a job, similar to the Earned Income Tax Credit that have benefited residents in the 50 states since 1975. In addition, Federal tax benefits to generate real investments in Puerto Rico can be designed similar to the provisions in Enterprise Zone acts and the Promise Zones legislative proposals of President Obama.

Bringing back Puerto Rico as a full partner into the Federal tax system would carry significant benefits to the People of Puerto Rico and the U.S. Treasury, but are not possible without your strong commitment to carry them through to the final budget agreement. As you know, there are formidable moneyed interests that benefit from using Puerto Rico as a tax heaven, and they would not give up the hugely inefficient tax deferral benefits without a fight. The almost 4 million disenfranchised

---

[1] See Caribbean Business, *"The real story behind Puerto Rico's low 40.6% labor-participation rate,"* May 10, 2011.

[2] Government Accountability Office, Tax Policy, *Analysis of Certain Potential Effects of Extending Federal Income Taxation to Puerto Rico,* GGD–96–127.

50

U.S. citizens in Puerto Rico count on your support to secure our equal rights and responsibilities.

THE STATUS ISSUE: THE 2012 PLEBISCITE AND STATEHOOD

Regarding the status issue, as you well know, statehood won the 2012 plebiscite. In that same election, with the same officials, in the same voting areas, with the same requirements. People voted for the Governor, the Resident Commissioner, Legislators, Mayors who were elected and sit in their positions. No one challenged their victories or re-interpreted them.

However, I should not have been surprised when the results were challenged by the spokespersons and hired guns from the economic powers that rule the island, among them a well-known Republican corporate lobbyist who sent out a statement to Congress and others (Attached) against the results of statehood's win. It is not the first time he does this, but then who wouldn't, if you're getting paid to the tune of >$2.745 million, just from Puerto Rico. I am sure there is even more $$$ to fight attacks against offshore corporations from their "corporate clients" with vested interest in keeping their business free of tax in the U.S. "FOREIGN" colony of U.S. Citizens in Puerto Rico.

Mr. Chairman, we thank for your support, and ask that Congress does not hold any more plebiscites on status.

We ask that you present a Puerto Rico statehood admission bill with the above terms and others that are considered fair, and ask the U.S. citizens in Puerto Rico to vote if they agree to Congress' terms and conditions.

I am submitting a draft admission act prepared by my constitutional counsel, Attorney Roberto Santana, which also includes what I call the Costas amendment, in honor of Attorney Luis Costas who first educated me on these issues. To get the CFC's on our side, (or rather off our backs), award the Corporations special tax incentives for a period of 20 years in the transition process. Then Congress and the people of Puerto Rico would negotiate the details of the transition process, which may or may not be submitted again to the people for final approval.

This is the way we designed it in the original Young bill.

C'MON FELLOW AMERICAN CITIZENS HERE IN CONGRESS!! LET'S DO THIS!

APPENDIX 1

Draft of Bill to Include Puerto Rico as Part of the United States

26 § 7701. Definitions

(a) When used in this title, where not otherwise distinctly expressed or manifestly incompatible with the intent thereof——

. . .

(4) Domestic

The term "domestic" when applied to a corporation or partnership means created or organized in the United States or under the law of the United States, or of any State, or Puerto Rico unless, in the case of a partnership, the Secretary provides otherwise by regulations.

. . .

(9) United States

The term "United States" when used in a geographical sense includes only the States, the District of Columbia and Puerto Rico.

PUERTO RICO—A "FOREIGN" TAX HAVEN IN THE U.S. BACKYARD

This brief describes the unexpected results of two Federal tax acts which have defined Puerto Rico's tax identity since it became a U.S. territory in 1898. The first law—the Revenue Act of 1921—classified Puerto Rico as a "foreign country" for tax purposes. The second piece—the Small Business Job Protection Act of 1996 Act—eliminated the main Federal tax incentive, known as Section 936, that the U.S. Congress used to promote new manufacturing jobs and investments in Puerto Rico until 1996.

What remained untouched after 1996 was Puerto Rico's "foreign" tax label, which was embraced by former Section 936 firms in order to obtain the benefits of tax deferral, converting to Controlled Foreign Corporations (CFCs). Unlike the former Section 936 program, however, the CFCs in Puerto Rico do not have to create jobs and generate real investments to benefit from tax deferral, and the U.S. Treasury does not have formal indicators to measure their cost effectiveness. This brief takes a first step to restore accountability and transparency for the CFCs in Puerto Rico, providing the evidence to assess growing CFC Federal tax benefits at a time of decreasing jobs and investments in Puerto Rico.

Section 1—Controlled Foreign Corporations (CFCs) in Puerto Rico

Puerto Rico has been an unincorporated territory of the United States under the jurisdiction of the U.S. Congress since the Spanish-American War of 1898.[3] Although major U.S. taxes apply in Puerto Rico as in the 50 states, e.g. Social Security taxes, for income tax purposes the U.S. Congress has excluded Puerto Rico since 1921 from the definition of "United States".[4] As a result, although Puerto Rico belongs to the United States and most of its residents are U.S. citizens, the income earned in Puerto Rico is considered "foreign-source income" and Puerto Rico corporations are considered "foreign." This category includes the CFCs with a U.S. parent entity, which are analyzed in this brief.

The 1921 Revenue Act also created the predecessor of the IRC Section 936, which became the preferred alternative to operate a U.S. subsidiary in the Island because it possessed two ideal features of a tax haven: Puerto Rico-source income was spared 100 percent of the U.S. Federal tax and it was subject to a minuscule P.R. tax, right inside the U.S. borders.[5]

U.S. electronic and pharmaceutical firms with significant intangible assets tried to maximize their tax benefits in Puerto Rico, engaging in transfer pricing practices which spawned important court cases and scathing U.S. Treasury reports. In order to curtail the abuses of Section 936 firms, Congress in 1993 tied tax benefits to payroll and depreciation expenses, in an effort to channel more of the Section 936 benefits to the U.S. citizens residing in Puerto Rico.

Finally, the U.S. Congress replaced Section 936 with a temporary Section 30A credit, and initiated a 10-year phase out of existing 936 subsidiaries. This momentous decision has created a massive conversion of Section 936 U.S. corporations to CFC status, and left U.S. Treasury without a congressional reporting mandate and performance indicators to assess the tax effectiveness and efficiency of CFCs in Puerto Rico.

The CFC conversions have triggered a significant increase in CFC activity in Puerto Rico, shown in Tables 1 to 5:

- There was a 122 percent increase in the reported Earnings and Profits (E&P) of CFCs in Puerto Rico, to $6.6 billion in 2008, which is the most recent year of available CFC data (Table 1).
- The average tax rate of CFCs in Puerto Rico was 3.9 percent in 2008, which was 10.2 percent lower than the average tax rate by CFCs operating in the world in 2008 (Table 2).
- The U.S. corporations with CFCs in Puerto Rico received in just 3 years $3.5 billion of tax benefits, relative to the 35 percent tax rate of U.S. domestic firms (Table 3).
- There was a wide variation in tax rates across industries. Manufacturing CFCs in Puerto Rico had a 2.3 percent tax rate, compared to the 14.9 percent tax rate of CFCs in finance (Table 4).
- The distribution of the tax benefits of CFCs is most likely highly concentrated in a few specific firms with significant intangible patents, trademarks and copyrights. Congressional investigators found that one CFC reported $4 billion in profits, and provided 177 direct jobs, or $22.5 million per job.

IRS and Congressional investigations have started to uncover significant transfer pricing abuses that lie behind the growing trend in earnings of U.S. CFCs in Puerto Rico. As early as 1997, the IRS designated Section 936 conversions to CFCs as a

---

[3] The Web site www.puertoricoreport.com provides summaries of Federal commissions that examined Puerto Rico's territorial status subject to Congressional powers.

[4] IRC Sec 7701(a)(9) defines the term "United States" in a geographical sense to include "only the States and the District of Columbia." In contrast, *The Revenue Act of 1916* (Part III, Sec. 15), defines the word "State" or "United States" to include any Territory, the District of Columbia, Porto Rico, and the Philippine Islands. *The Revenue Act of 1921* (Title I, Sec. 1), excludes Porto Rico and the Philippines from the definition of the "United States."

[5] See Joint Committee on Taxation, *An Overview of Special Tax Rules Related to Puerto Rico and an Analysis of the Tax and Economic Policy Implications of Recent Legislative Opinions*, (JCX–24–06), June 23, 2006.

Tier I issue, with high potential compliance risks.[6] In 2011 IRS sent notices of deficiency to Medtronic for $958 million and to Boston Scientific for $452 million over their Section 936 conversions to CFC status.[7]

In 2012 the staff of the U.S. Senate Permanent Subcommittee on Investigations analyzed the complex layers of tax haven subsidiaries created by Microsoft to minimize its tax on sales of products manufactured in Puerto Rico and sold in the United States. According to the congressional report, in 2011 the CFC of Microsoft in Puerto Rico reported $4 billion in profits, and provided 177 direct jobs earning an average salary of $44,000 a year, or $22.5 million per person. This example shows the low ineffectiveness of a specific CFC in Puerto Rico. Ideally, the U.S. Treasury should conduct an in-depth examination of the whole program of CFC tax incentives in Puerto Rico, as was done of the Section 936 tax program.

Table 1: Assets, Receipts, Earnings & Profits, and Taxes of CFCs in Puerto Rico

Indicators	Years			Percent change '04 - '08
$ in billion	'04	'06	'08	
Number of CFCs in PR	395	401	423	7%
Total assets	$25.9	$26.7	$31.4	21%
Total receipts	$17.2	$26.7	$27.7	61%
Earnings and profits (E&P) before income taxes	**$2.996**	**$2.756**	**$6.639**	**122%**
Income taxes	$0.265	$0.275	$0.262	0%
Average tax rate	**8.9%**	**10.0%**	**3.9%**	

Source: IRS Statistics of Income (SOI) Bulletin, "Controlled Foreign Corporations", Table 3, Summer 2008, Winter 2011, Winter 2013.

Note: Data are based on the SOI corporate sample. Since 2004 this sample is far more inclusive than earlier SOI studies of CFCs.

Table 2: Average tax rates of CFCs in Puerto Rico and in other countries

Average tax rates	'04	'06	'08
CFCs in Puerto Rico	**8.9%**	**10.0%**	**3.9%**
CFCs in other countries	15.7%	16.4%	14.1%
Difference in tax rates	(6.8%)	(6.4%)	(10.2%)

Note: Average tax rate is defined as income tax divided by E&P before income taxes.

Source: IRS Statistics of Income Bulletin, "Controlled Foreign Corporations", Summer 2008, Winter 2011, Winter 2013.

[6] See *Audit Guidelines Related to Section 936 Conversion Issues* in www.irs.gov.
[7] See *Puerto Rico Tax Break Shifts to Cayman Islands*, in www.bloomberg.com, and docket number 006944–11 in www.taxcourt.gov.

Table 3: Tax benefits of operating in Puerto Rico as CFC, compared to operating as a U.S. domestic firm, annually and average figures in latest 3 years

	'04	'06	'08	Total, 3 yrs
Top US corporate tax rate	35.0%	35.0%	35.0%	
Minus: PR CFC average tax rate	**8.9%**	**10.0%**	**3.9%**	
Equals: tax rate advantage of PR CFCs over domestic US firms	26.1%	25.0%	31.1%	
Multiplied by: Earnings & profits of PR CFCs before income tax (millions)	$2,996	$2,756	$6,639	**$12,391**
Equals: Federal tax benefit of CFCs in Puerto Rico over domestic US firms (millions)	**$782**	**$689**	**$2,065**	**$3,536**

Note: Author's calculation, based on data reported in IRS Statistics of Income Bulletin, "Controlled Foreign Corporations", Summer 2008, Winter 2011, Winter 2013.

Table 4: Average tax rates of CFCs in Puerto Rico in 2008

Industrial sector	# of PR CFCs	Earnings and profits before tax ($million)	Average tax rate in 2008
Goods production (manufacture)	101	1,352	2.3%
Finance, insurance, real estate	69	426	14.9%
Distribution and transportation	108	259	37.6%
Services	105	4,550	1.4%
Other sectors	40	53	14.9%
Total	423	6,640	3.9%

Note: Average tax rate is defined as income tax divided by E&P before income taxes.

Source: IRS Statistics of Income Bulletin, "Controlled Foreign Corporations", Summer 2008, Winter 2011, Winter 2013.

Given the trend in Federal tax benefits received by CFCs operating in Puerto Rico, it is appropriate to assess how this Federal tax program has contributed to the economic well-being of the almost 4 million U.S. citizens in Puerto Rico. Measures of effectiveness and efficiency of the tax benefits of manufacturing CFCs are discussed in the next section of this brief.

Section 2—Measuring the cost effectiveness of the CFCs in Puerto Rico

CFCs were introduced in 1921 in Puerto Rico "primarily to help U.S. corporations compete with foreign firms in the Philippines."[8] There is no question that for U.S. multinationals the benefits of tax deferral can be significant, since indefinite deferral of U.S. tax liability generates a complete tax exemption on the foreign-source income. As was shown in Section 1 of this brief, tax deferral is a powerful tax tool to enhance the financial capacity of U.S. multinationals to compete against all firms, especially the domestic U.S. firms that pay the 35 percent maximum Federal corporate tax rate.

However, utilizing the 1921 tax law criterion—"help U.S. businesses to compete in foreign countries against foreign firms"—is not appropriate for determining the CFC benefits in Puerto Rico for three reasons: the Island is a territory of the United States, almost all of its 3.7 million residents are U.S. citizens, and the 423 CFCs in Puerto Rico represent less than 1 percent of the 83,642 CFCs in the World.

Congress did introduce a different objective when it enacted Section 936 tax benefits for Puerto Rico, namely, "to assist the U.S. possession in obtaining

---

[8] Joint Committee on Taxation, JCX–24–06, op. cit., page 50.

employment producing investments by U.S. corporations."[9] In order to obtain a precise estimate of tax benefits per employee it is necessary to obtain firm-specific tax and jobs data, which is not available to the public.

An imprecise estimate of tax benefits per employee is obtained with U.S. Bureau of census data of manufacturing establishments in Puerto Rico, which are owned by CFCs and others. For example, in 2008 there were 2,064 manufacturing establishments with 106,132 employees in Puerto Rico, shown in Table 5. Estimates of the average CFC earnings before income taxes of manufacturing establishments range from $12,739 (if all jobs are assigned to the CFCs) to $25,477 per employee (if 50 percent of the jobs are assigned to CFCs) in 2008. These averages, in contrast to the $22 million per job earned by Microsoft Puerto Rico in 2011, show that the distribution of the tax benefits of CFCs is most likely highly concentrated in a few specific firms with significant intangible patents, trademarks and copyrights.

Table 5: Manufacturing Operations in Puerto Rico, Tax Benefits of CFCs and Jobs, 2008

Sources		2008
Census	Number of manufacturing establishments in PR	2,064
	Employees in manufacturing establishments	**106,132**
SOI	Earnings before income taxes of manufacturing CFCs (million)	$1,352
	CFC earnings before income tax per employee in manufacturing establishments in Puerto Rico	
	100% of jobs were in US CFCs	$12,739
	50% of jobs were in US CFCs	$25,477

Sources: (1) U.S. Bureau of Census, *County Business Patterns*, published annually. (2) Federal tax benefits estimated using IRS SOI Bulletin, "Controlled Foreign Corporations", published in even years.

Keeping Puerto Rico as a "foreign" country inside the United States undermines the U.S. Federal tax base and creates unfair competition against local communities in the 50 states. For example, in 2010 the Puerto Rico government imposed a 4 percent excise tax on CFCs in Puerto Rico in order to pay for a significant reduction in income taxes at the local level. Normally, excise taxes cannot be used as foreign tax credits that reduce the U.S. tax liability dollar for dollar. However, in the case of the Puerto Rico's 4 percent excise tax on the U.S. CFCs, the IRS took the position that it would not challenge if U.S. corporations claim a U.S. foreign tax credit. In contrast, taxes imposed in the 50 states can be deducted when calculating Federal income tax, provided they are attributable to the conduct of the corporation's business. Effectively, the U.S. Treasury subsidized Puerto Rico's 4 percent excise tax increase almost dollar for dollar. This tax expenditure is not available in the 50 states.

How do these estimated Federal cost estimates compare to another Federal credit that is directly linked to job creation, namely, the Earned Income Tax Credit (EITC), is discussed in the next section of this brief.

Section 3—Incorporating Puerto Rico Residents into the Federal Income Tax System and I.R.C. Section 933

Congress in 1917 granted U.S. citizenship to individuals born in Puerto Rico. Thus, a person born in Puerto Rico is subject to the U.S. tax laws. However, Section 933 of the IRC exempts from U.S. taxation the Puerto Rico-source income obtained by bona fide residents of Puerto Rico. Some observers have expressed the opinion that the residents of Puerto Rico are better off because Federal income tax laws do not apply in the Island. This opinion is not correct for two reasons:

1. The Federal income tax provides job incentives that are lacking in Federal direct spending programs. For example, the exclusion of Puerto Rico residents from the Federal income tax has prevented almost 60 percent of working families from receiving the Federal Earned Income Tax Credit (EITCs). The Federal income tax could be used as an effective tool to increase Puerto Rico's

---

[9] Joint Committee on Taxation, JCX-24-06, op. cit., page 50.

40 percent labor force participation rate, which is the lowest in the United States.[10]

2. The introduction of the Federal income tax, with the administrative support of the Internal Revenue Service, would increase the effectiveness of the local tax administration in Puerto Rico. Local tax auditors in the Department of Hacienda have experienced a 50 percent decrease in the last 6 years, at the time when the underground economy in Puerto Rico has grown to about 25 percent of the market economy.

Previous congressional studies have already shown the benefits of participating in the Federal tax system. For example, GAO in 1996 found that if IRC tax rules are applied to residents of Puerto Rico, the average EITC earned by eligible taxpayers would be $1,494, taxpayers would owe around $623 million in Federal income tax before taking into account the earned income tax credit (EITC), and the aggregate amount of EITC would total $574 million. About 59 percent of the population filing individual income tax returns would earn some EITC, and 41 percent of the households filing income tax returns would have positive Federal income tax liabilities, greater than the EITC received. Thus, the introduction of the Federal income tax in Puerto Rico for individuals would generate a wealth transfer from higher-income individuals who would pay Federal income taxes, to lower-income earners who would receive a refundable credit.[11]

CONCLUSION

This brief has demonstrated the importance of incorporating Puerto Rico back into the United States for income tax purposes. This fundamental change is necessary to protect the U.S. tax base from the abuses in the ill-defined CFC regime in Puerto Rico. Furthermore, the inclusion of individual taxpayers into the Federal income tax regime would allow families in the Island to receive significant incentives that are likely to increase Puerto Rico's low labor force participation rate, and restore economic growth in the Island.

* * * * *

DRAFT ADMISSION ACT
Prepared by Attorney Roberto Santana

Admission of State

Section 1

AN ACT

To provide for the admission of the Commonwealth of Puerto Rico into the Union

Be it enacted by the Senate and House of Representatives of the United States of America in Congress assembled, That, subject to the provisions of this Act, Congress consents that the territory properly included within and rightfully belonging to the territory of Puerto Rico, officially known and hereinafter referred to as the "Commonwealth of Puerto Rico," may be erected into a new State, with the consent of the existing Government in order that the same may by admitted as one of the States of this Union on an equal footing with the other States in all respects whatever, subject to the affirmative vote of the eligible voters of the Commonwealth of Puerto Rico accepting the terms and conditions of this Act.

Territory

Section 2

The official name of the State of Puerto Rico shall remain to be "Commonwealth of Puerto Rico" and the newly admitted State shall consist of all its islands, together

---

[10] See Caribbean Business, *"The real story behind Puerto Rico's low 40.6% labor-participation rate,"* May 10, 2011.
[11] Government Accountability Office, Tax Policy, *Analysis of Certain Potential Effects of Extending Federal Income Taxation to Puerto Rico,* GGD–96–127.

with their appurtenant reefs and territorial waters, including but not limited to the main island of Puerto Rico, and the islands of Vieques, Culebra, Mona, Monito, Ratones, Caja de Muertos, Palomino, Palominito, Luis Peña, Lobos, Icacos, Isleta Marina and other smaller islands, atolls and reefs presently under the jurisdiction of the Commonwealth of Puerto Rico and including a ten and thirty five hundreths of a mile (10.35) mile Exclusive Economic Zone (EEZ) which is the sea zone over which the Commonwealth of Puerto Rico has special rights over the exploration and use of marine resources and stretching from the seaward edge of the Commonwealth of Puerto Rico's territorial sea out to 10.35 nautical miles from its coast and including the territorial sea and the continental shelf beyond the 10.35 nautical mile limit.

Constitution

Section 3

Congress finds that the Constitution of the Commonwealth of Puerto Rico is republican in form; it is not repugnant to the Constitution of the United States and the principles of the Declaration of Independence and is the functional equivalent of a state constitution.

Agreement with United States

Section 4

The Commonwealth of Puerto Rico and its people, by the affirmative vote of the eligible voters of the Commonwealth of Puerto Rico accepting the terms and conditions of this Act do agree and declare that they forever disclaim all right and title to any lands or other property not granted or confirmed to the State or its political subdivisions by or under the authority of this Act, the right or title to which is held by the United States or is subject to disposition by the United States, and to any lands or other property, (including fishing rights); that all such lands or other property, belonging to the United States shall be and remain under the absolute jurisdiction and control of the United States until disposed of under its authority, except to such extent as the Congress has prescribed or may hereafter prescribe. Provided, That nothing contained in this Act shall recognize, deny, enlarge, impair, or otherwise affect any claim against the United States, and any such claim shall be governed by the laws of the United States applicable thereto; and nothing in this Act is intended or shall be construed as a finding, interpretation, or construction by the Congress that any law applicable thereto authorizes, establishes, recognizes, or confirms the validity or invalidity of any such claim, and the determination of the applicability or effect of any law to any such claim shall be unaffected by anything in this Act: And provided further, That no taxes shall be imposed by said State upon any lands or other property now owned or hereafter acquired by the United States, except to such extent as the Congress has prescribed or may hereafter prescribe.

Title to Property; Land Grants; Reservation of Lands; Public School Support; Submerged Lands

Section 5

The Commonwealth of Puerto Rico and its political subdivisions, respectively, shall have and retain title to all property, real and personal, within the Commonwealth of Puerto Rico or any of the subdivisions. Except as provided herein, the United States shall retain title to all property, real and personal, to which it has title, including public lands. Provided that:

(a) Except as provided in subsection (c) of this section, the Commonwealth of Puerto Rico and its political subdivisions, as the case may be, shall retain title of its properties before the passing of this Act and its subdivisions in those lands and other properties in which the Territory and its subdivisions now hold title.

(b) Except as provided in subsection (c) and (d) of this section, the United States grants to the Commonwealth of Puerto Rico, effective upon its admission into the Union, the United States' title to all the public lands and other public property, in the Island of Vieques after certification by the secretary of the Interior that any and all of such lands have been cleaned of all debris and unexploded ordinance used by the Armed Forces of the United States in training of the Military, title to which is held by the United States immediately prior to the Commonwealth of Puerto Rico's admission into the Union. The grant hereby made shall be in lieu of any and all grants provided for new States by provisions of law other than this Act, and such grants shall not extend to the Commonwealth of Puerto Rico.

(c) Any lands and other properties that, on the date Puerto Rico is admitted into the Union, are set aside pursuant to law for the use of the United States under any (1) Act of Congress, (2) Executive order, (3) proclamation of the President, or (4) proclamation of the Governor of Puerto Rico shall remain the property of the United States subject only to the limitations, if any, imposed under (1), (2), (3), or (4), as the case may be.

(d) Any public lands or other public property that is conveyed to the Commonwealth of Puerto Rico by subsection (b) of this section but that, immediately prior to the admission of said State into the Union, is controlled by the United States pursuant to permit, license, of permission, written or verbal, from the Commonwealth of Puerto Rico or any department thereof may, at any time during the five years following the admission of Puerto Rico into the Union, be set aside by Act of Congress or by Executive Order of the President, made pursuant to law, for the use of the United States, and the lands or property so set aside shall, subject only to valid rights then existing, be the property of the United States.

(e) Within five years from the date Commonwealth of Puerto Rico is admitted into the Union, each Federal agency having control over any land or property that is retained by the United States pursuant to subsections (c) and (d) of this section shall report to the President the facts regarding its continued need for such land or property, and if the President determines that the land or property is no longer needed by the United States it shall be conveyed to the Commonwealth of Puerto Rico.

(f) The lands granted to the Commonwealth of Puerto Rico by subsection (b) of this section and public lands retained by the United States under subsections (c) and (d) and later conveyed to the State under subsection (e), together with the proceeds from the sale or other disposition of any such lands and the income therefrom, shall be held by said State as a public trust for the support of the public schools and other public educational institutions, for the betterment of the conditions of Puerto Ricans. Such lands, proceeds, and income shall be managed and disposed of for one or more of the foregoing purposes in such manner as the constitution and laws of said State may provide, and their use for any other object shall constitute a breach of trust for which suit may be brought by the United States. The schools and other educational institutions supported, in whole or in part, out of such public trust shall forever remain under the exclusive control of said State; and no part of the proceeds or income from the lands granted under this Act shall be used for the support of any sectarian or denominational school, college, or university.

(g) As used in this Act, the term 'lands and other properties' includes public lands and other public property, and the term 'public lands and other public property' means, and is limited to, the lands and properties that were ceded to the United States by Spain under the Treaty of Paris of 1898, or that have been acquired in exchange for lands or properties so ceded.

(h) All laws of the United States reserving to the United States the free use or enjoyment of property which vests in or is conveyed to the Commonwealth of Puerto Rico or its political subdivisions pursuant to subsection (a), (b), or (e) of this section or reserving the right to alter, amend, or repeal laws relating thereto shall cease to be effective upon the admission of the Commonwealth of Puerto Rico into the Union.

(i) The Submerged Lands Act of 1953 (Public Law 31, Eighty-third Congress, first session; 67 Stat. 29) and the Outer Continental Shelf Lands Act of 1953 (Public Law 212, Eighty-third Congress, first session, 67 Stat. 462) shall be applicable to the Commonwealth of Puerto Rico, and the said State shall have the same rights as do existing States thereunder. (As amended Pub. L. 86–624, Sec. 41, July 12, 1960, 74 Stat. 422, Pub. L. 95–372, Title II, § 202, 92 Stat. 634; Apr. 7, 1986, Pub. L. 99–272, Title VIII, § 8002, 100 Stat. 148)

Assumption of Public Debt

Section 6

For the purposes of furthering the development of the new State, and the expansion of its economy, and in exchange of the citizens of the Commonwealth of Puerto Rico acquiring as taxpaying citizens of the United States their corresponding share of the National Debt of the United States, the Public Debt of the Commonwealth of Puerto Rico, as of the date of Admission, is hereby acquired by the Treasury of the United States and shall be paid according to its terms and as it becomes due.

Presidential Certification

Section 7

Upon enactment of this Act, it shall be the duty of the President of the United States, not later than 30 days thereafter, to certify such fact to the Governor of the Commonwealth of Puerto Rico and to the presidents of the Senate and of the House of Representatives of Puerto Rico. Thereupon, (1) the legislature of the Commonwealth of Puerto Rico shall enact legislation to provide for the vote by the eligible voters of the Commonwealth of Puerto Rico as defined by law to accept or reject the terms and conditions of this Act, by simple majority vote, which referendum will take place not later than 180 days after the Presidential Certification made pursuant to this section and (2) The State Elections Commission of Puerto Rico is authorized to provide for a vote on the admission of Puerto Rico into the Union as a State within one hundred and eighty days from the date of the Presidential Certification made pursuant to this section, in accordance with rules and regulations determined by the Commission, including qualifications for voter eligibility. The ballot shall ask the following question: "Shall Puerto Rico be admitted as a State of the United States pursuant to the Act of Congress dated [the date of this Act]?
Yes ___ No ___."

The funds made available pursuant to Public Law 113–76 may be used to conduct the vote.

The Governor of the Commonwealth of Puerto Rico is hereby authorized and directed to take such action as may be necessary or appropriate to insure the submission of said proposition to the people. The return of the votes cast on said referendum shall be made by the election officers directly to the State Elections Commission, which entity shall certify the results to the Governor. The Governor shall certify the results of said referendum, as so ascertained, to the President of the United States, the Speaker of the House of Representatives, and the President Pro Tempore of the Senate.

Election, Certification, Proclamation, Laws in Effect

Section 8

(a) Upon the affirmative vote of the eligible voters of the Commonwealth of Puerto Rico accepting the offer of Statehood, the Governor of the Commonwealth of Puerto Rico shall call for the holding of a Primary Election for Federal office and a General Election to elect such federal elected official, on dates to be fixed by the Governor of the Commonwealth of Puerto Rico. Provided, that the elections for Federal office shall not be held later than the date already legislated by the laws of the Commonwealth for the holding of the next regular General Elections that are held on November on the same year as that of the Presidential Elections of the United States and at such elections there shall be elected 2 Senators and 5 Representatives, each of whom shall first take office on the first day of the next Congress commencing immediately after said election. The Legislature of Puerto Rico shall delineate and enact the corresponding congressional districts. The officers required to be elected as provided in this section shall be chosen by the eligible voters of the Commonwealth of Puerto Rico. Such elections shall be held, and the qualifications of voters thereat shall be, as prescribed by the Constitution of the Commonwealth of Puerto Rico for the election of members of the State legislature. The Legislature of Puerto Rico shall delineate and enact the corresponding congressional districts.

The returns thereof shall be made and certified in such manner as the constitution and laws of the Commonwealth of Puerto Rico may prescribe. The Governor of the Commonwealth of Puerto Rico shall certify the results of said elections to the President of the United States, the Speaker of the House of Representatives, and the President Pro Tempore of the Senate.

(b) In the election of Senators from Puerto Rico pursuant to this section, the 2 Senate offices shall be separately identified and designated, and no person may be a candidate for both offices. No such identification or designation of either of the offices shall refer to or be taken to refer to the terms of such offices, or in any way impair the privilege of the Senate to determine the class to which each of the Senators elected shall be assigned.

(c) The President of the United States, once notified by the Governor of the election of the federal officials prescribed pursuant to this section, upon certification of the returns of the election of the officers required to be elected as provided herein, shall thereupon issue his proclamation announcing the results of said election as so ascertained. Upon the issuance of said proclamation by the President, the Commonwealth of Puerto Rico shall be deemed admitted into the Union as provided in this Act.

(d) Until Puerto Rico is so admitted into the Union, all of the officers of the Commonwealth of Puerto Rico, including its Resident Commissioner, shall continue to discharge the duties of their respective offices. Upon the issuance of said proclamation by the President of the United States and the admission of the Commonwealth of Puerto Rico into the Union, the officers elected at said election, and qualified under the provisions of the constitution and laws of said State, shall proceed to exercise all the functions pertaining to their offices in or under or by authority of the government of said State, and officers not required to be elected at said initial election shall be selected or continued in office as provided by the constitution and laws of said State.

(e) The State Elections Commission of Puerto Rico shall certify the election of the Senators and Representative in the manner required by law, and the said Senators and Representative shall be entitled to be admitted to seats in Congress and to all the rights and privileges of Senators and Representatives of other States in the Congress of the United States.

(f) Upon admission of the Commonwealth of Puerto Rico into the Union as herein provided, all of the territorial laws then in force in the Commonwealth of Puerto Rico shall be and continue in full force and effect throughout said State except as modified or changed by this Act, or by the Constitution of the State, or as thereafter modified or changed by the legislature of the State. All of the laws of the United States shall have the same force and effect within said State as elsewhere within the United States. As used in this paragraph, the term "territorial laws" includes (in addition to laws enacted by the Legislature of Puerto Rico) all laws or parts thereof enacted by Congress, the validity of which is dependent solely upon the authority of Congress to provide for the government of prior to the admission of the Commonwealth of Puerto Rico into the Union, and the term "laws of the United States" includes all laws or parts thereof enacted by Congress that (1) apply to or within Puerto Rico at the time of the admission of the Commonwealth of Puerto Rico into the Union, (2) are not "Territorial laws" as defined in this paragraph, and (3) are not in conflict with any other provisions of this Act.

House of Representatives Membership

Section 9

(a) The Commonwealth of Puerto Rico upon its admission into the Union shall be entitled to the number of Representatives mentioned in Section 8 of this Act until the taking effect of the next reapportionment, and such Representatives shall be in addition to the membership of the House of Representatives as now prescribed by law: Provided, That such temporary increase in the membership shall not operate to either increase or decrease the permanent membership of the House of Representatives as prescribed in the Act of August 8, 1911 (37 Stat. 13) nor shall such temporary increase affect the basis of apportionment established by the Act of November 15, 1941 (55 Stat. 761; 2 U.S.C., section 2a), for the Eighty-third Congress and each Congress thereafter.

(b) Effective on the date on which a Representative from Puerto Rico first takes office in accordance with this subsection, the Office of the Resident Commissioner to the United States, as described in section 36 of the Act of March 2, 1917 (48 U.S.C. 891 et seq.), is terminated.

Continuation of Civil Cases and Criminal Proceedings

Section 10

No writ, action, indictment, cause, or proceeding pending in the United States District Court for the District of Puerto Rico on the date when said Territory shall become a State, and no case pending in an appellate court upon appeal from the United States District Court for the district of Puerto Rico at the time said Territory shall become a State, shall abate by the admission of the Commonwealth of Puerto Rico into the Union, but the same shall be transferred and proceeded with as hereinafter provided.

All civil causes of action and all criminal offenses which shall have arisen or been committed prior to the admission of said State, but as to which no suit, action, or prosecution shall be pending at the date of such admission, shall be subject to prosecution in the appropriate State courts or in the United States District Court for the District of Puerto Rico in like manner, to the same extent, and with like right of appellate review, as if said State had been created and said courts had been established prior to the accrual of said causes of action or the commission of such offenses; and such of said criminal offenses as shall have been committed against the laws of the Territory shall be tried and punished by the appropriate courts of said State, and such as shall have been committed against the laws of the United States shall be tried and punished in the United States District Court for the District of Puerto Rico.

Appeals

Section 11

All appeals taken from the United States District Court District of Puerto Rico to the Supreme Court of the United States or the United States Court of Appeals for the First Circuit, previous to the admission of Puerto Rico as a State, shall be prosecuted to final determination as though this Act had not been passed. All cases in which final judgment has been rendered in such district court, and in which appeals might be had except for the admission of such State, may still be sued out, taken, and prosecuted to the Supreme Court of the United States or the United States Court of Appeals for the First Circuit under the provisions of then existing law, and there held and determined in like manner; and in either case, the Supreme Court of the United States, or the United States Court of Appeals, in the event of reversal, shall remand the said cause to either the Puerto Rico Supreme Court, or the United States District Court for the District of Puerto Rico, as the case may require: Provided, That the time allowed by existing law for appeals from the district court for said Territory shall not be enlarged thereby.

Continuation of Cases

Section 12

All causes pending or determined in the United States District Court for the District of Puerto Rico at the time of the admission of Puerto Rico as a State shall continue under the jurisdiction of the United States District Court for the District of Puerto Rico for final disposition and enforcement in the same manner as is now provided by law with reference to the judgments and decrees. All other causes pending or determined in the State Courts of the Commonwealth of Puerto Rico at the time of the admission of Puerto Rico as a State shall continue under the jurisdiction of the State Courts of the Commonwealth of Puerto Rico. All final judgments and decrees rendered in the United States District Court for the District of Puerto Rico may be reviewed by the Supreme Court of the United States or by the United States Court of Appeals for the First Circuit in the same manner as is now provided by law with reference to the judgments and decrees in existing United States district courts.

Retention of Jurisdiction and Appeals in State Court

Section 13

Jurisdiction of all cases pending or determined in the General Court of Justice of the Commonwealth of Puerto Rico shall devolve upon and be exercised by said court and, as such, it shall retain custody of all records, dockets, journals, and files pertaining to such cases. All appeals taken from the Supreme Court of Puerto Rico to the Supreme Court of the United States, previous to the admission of Puerto Rico as a State, shall be prosecuted to final determination as though this Act had not been passed. All cases in which final judgment has been rendered in such court, and in which appeals might be had except for the admission of such State, may still be sued out, taken, and prosecuted to the Supreme Court of the United States under the provisions of then existing law, and there held and determined in like manner; and in either case, the Supreme Court of the United States, in the event of reversal, shall remand the said cause to the Puerto Rico Supreme Court as the case may require: Provided, That the time allowed by existing law for appeals from the Supreme Court of Puerto Rico shall not be enlarged thereby.

Federal Reserve Act; Amendment

Section 14

The next to last sentence of the first paragraph of section 2 of the Federal Reserve Act (38 Stat. 251) as amended, is hereby amended by inserting after the word 'Hawaii' the words 'or Puerto Rico.'

Maritime Matters

Section 15

Nothing contained in this Act shall be construed as depriving the Federal Maritime Board of the exclusive jurisdiction heretofore conferred on it over common carriers engaged in transportation by water between any port in the Commonwealth of Puerto Rico and other ports in the United States, or possessions, or as conferring on the Interstate Commerce Commission jurisdiction over transportation by water between any such ports.

Taxation

Section 16

Upon the effective date of the Admission of the Commonwealth of Puerto Rico as the 51st State of the Union, those individuals and corporations then currently enjoying tax status and tax benefits existing under Puerto Rico Income, Gift and Estate Tax Statutes and the U.S. Internal Revenue Code on that date, shall continue in that status and with those benefits for a period of twenty (20) years from that effective date of Admission. The U.S. Internal Revenue Service shall promulgate such Rules and Regulations as may be deemed necessary and/or convenient in order to carry out this Statutory Provision.

Repeal

Section 17

All parts of the Puerto Rican Federal Relations Act, Pub. L. No. 81–600, 64 Stat. 3 19 (1950) (codified at 48 U.S.C. §§ 731b–731e (1994)) ("Public Law 600") and any remaining sections in effect of the Act of Apr. 12, 1900, 31 Stat. 77 ("Foraker Act") and of the Act of Mar. 2, 1917, 39 Stat. 961, as amended, ("the Puerto Rican Federal Relations Act," also popularly known as the "Jones Act"), which are in conflict with the provisions of this Act, are hereby repealed.

United States Citizenship
Section 18

Nothing contained in this Act shall operate to confer United States citizenship, nor to terminate citizenship heretofore lawfully acquired, nor restore citizenship heretofore lost under any law of the United States or under any treaty to which the United States may have been a party.

Separability
Section 19

If any provision of this Act, or any section, subsection, sentence, clause, phrase, or individual word, or the application thereof to any person or circumstance is held invalid, the validity of the remainder of the Act and of the application of any such provision, section, subsection, sentence, clause, phrase, or individual word to other persons and circumstances shall not be affected thereby.

General Amendment and General Repeal
Section 20

All Acts or parts of Acts referring to "the 50 states" shall be amended to read "the 51 states" and all such Acts or parts of Acts referring to the Islands and Territories of Guam, American Samoa, Northern Mariana Islands, Puerto Rico and the Virgin Islands shall be amended to exclude the words "Puerto Rico," whether such Acts or parts of Acts were passed by the legislature of Puerto Rico or by Congress.

All Acts or parts of Acts in conflict with the provisions of this Act, whether passed by the legislature of Puerto Rico or by Congress, are hereby repealed.

———

Mr. YOUNG. Thank you, Miriam.

I will recognize the Ranking Member, and he is going to yield to the good lady from Guam.

Mr. SABLAN. Yes, I am going to yield to the dean of those Members of Congress who don't have a vote. She is our dean.

[Laughter.]

Mr. YOUNG. Don't knock it.

Ms. BORDALLO. Thank you very much to our Ranking Member, Mr. Sablan, from the CNMI.

Mr. Chairman, there are four of us up here, territorial delegates. One is missing. I think she belongs—oh, she just—that is right. We are now complete. Five of us. And let me say this, and I want to go on record as saying that the life of a territorial delegate in the U.S. Congress is the most frustrating job you would have ever expected it to be. When your colleagues are going over to vote, you are standing there watching them. And they say, "Why don't you go to vote?"

I said, "Well, we don't vote." Oh, that is right. So, ladies and gentlemen, I sympathize in everything that is being said here. Guam is in the same boat. We don't have 3 or 4 million people; we are very small. But when you are not able to vote for the U.S. President, as a citizen, and you cannot vote for amendments and final passage in the U.S. Congress, yet we sit in the committees, that is a frustrating position. And I have been here 13 years; I know all about it.

Now, the Governor, in his opening testimony, he asked three questions. My answer to those three questions is yes, yes, yes. You are absolutely right. Or—no? Would it have been no? What was the question again, Governor? It was yes, right?

Mr. BARCELÓ. Yes. It was a yes.

Ms. BORDALLO. It was a yes. OK.

Mr. BARCELÓ. It was a yes.

Ms. BORDALLO. I want to be sure that I am on the right side. [Laughter.]

Ms. BORDALLO. Thank you, Governor. Yes, yes, yes. All right.

I do have a question here for Mr. Vilá. I am interested in your views on the idea of mutual consent. As I understand it, mutual consent between the United States and Puerto Rico is still being discussed among the people of Puerto Rico, as part of an opinion for political status. How would mutual consent be formulated to satisfy objections that it is unconstitutional, or to meet any objections by the Department of Justice?

Mr. VILÁ. In my written statement, and in the documents that I included, I go a little bit deeper on that. I think that approach is not the right one. And I do say with total honesty and respect, I think that so far we have been discussing this from a political, legal view. I think it is about time just to discuss the economic relationship between Puerto Rico and the United States.

I firmly believe that statehood, economically, is not the alternative, and we can go into deeper discussion on that. It is in my written statement, I don't want to waste your time. But I firmly believe it is not a good solution for Puerto Rico or for the United States either. I firmly believe independence is not the right economic answer to our situation, and I firmly believe doing nothing, the status quo, is also not the alternative.

I believe that we need to sit down and come up with a new economic arrangement. What is the problem? The problem is that Puerto Rico is, and has always been, a developing economy. But then we have to play by the rules of the most developed economy in the world, which is the U.S. economy. And when you apply the rules of the most developed economy to a developing economy, you have the problem we have. And if we become a state, it will be even worse, because you will apply the tax rules of the most developing economy to a still developing economy.

So, in that sense, my approach is let's reach an agreement on a new kind of economic relationship, and then, based on that, let's reach an agreement in what the mayor called, ELA Soberano, estado libre asociado soberano, a new political arrangement, clearly non-colonial and non-territorial.

Ms. BORDALLO. Thank you very much.

Mr. Chairman, thank you for being so supportive of our issues. And, Ranking Member Sablan, thank you for the time.

Mr. BARCELÓ. Mr. Chairman, could I——

Mr. YOUNG. You have 21 seconds, then I have to let her ask questions.

Mr. BARCELÓ. Could I address, myself, to some of the things that he has mentioned about the economy?

Mr. YOUNG. We will get that next time.

Mr. BARCELÓ. OK.

Mr. YOUNG. Madam Vice Chair.

Mrs. RADEWAGEN. Thank you, Mr. Chairman. I too want to welcome the panel of very distinguished public servants. I see Governor Romero, who was a colleague of my dad when they served together as Governors of American Samoa and Puerto Rico, respectively; Governor Luis Fortuño, a former Member of this body and a colleague on the RNC. Warm welcome to all of you.

When I spoke in this committee room at a hearing earlier this year, I used the term "colonialism by another name." Well, a three-judge panel gave it another name: "Cultural imperialism." That Federal court of appeals just rejected the argument lawyers made in a case claiming the national citizenship clause in the Constitution applies in American Samoa and all other unincorporated U.S. territories.

So once again, the courts have confirmed that U.S. nationals in American Samoa and U.S. nationals from Puerto Rico and the three other unincorporated territories are required to relocate to a state of the Union to secure full and equal rights and duties of U.S. citizenship. That means full and equal rights of national citizenship, including the fundamental right of government by consent through voting rights in the Federal elections are guaranteed only through citizenship in a state, rather than a territory.

So, for residents of all five unincorporated territories who don't move to a state, the status of a U.S. national in American Samoa and a U.S. citizen in a territory is constitutionally the same, with only those rights under the Constitution and Federal law confirmed by Congress and Federal statutes enacted under the territorial power.

I have a question for Governor Fortuño. Given the predicament for the territories and for Congress due to the twisted saga of unincorporated territory status, do you agree that the best path forward is for Congress to support self-determination for each territory, based on status options that are legally valid, politically feasible, and compatible with the freely expressed wishes of a majority in votes held whenever each territory decides to seek a change of status?

Also, would you care to comment on the consistent Federal court rulings that confirm full and equal rights of U.S. national citizenship that include that Federal voting rights are attainable only through state citizenship, and what it means for those citizens in Puerto Rico who democratically have expressed a desire for new status with equal rights of national citizenship that includes Federal voting rights?

Mr. FORTUÑO. Thank you, and I commend you for raising this very important question. And, it is an honor to see you sitting up there on the dais.

As you very well state, there is a situation that was court-created of a so-called unincorporated territory. And what it means is that it grants Congress carte blanche to essentially do whatever it wants with the U.S. citizens residing in the territories. Initially, it was only applicable to territories with non-citizens. But it has been extended and applied to territories where American citizens reside, American citizens that actually have served with valor and courage in every single war, in our case, since 1917.

The only way to address this situation whereby our constitutional rights are never the same if we live in a territory is to either move to one of the 50 states or become a state. In order to attain that, there ought to be, in my opinion, number one, a process by which majority rules in the territory, in terms of the terms that are acceptable, but also in terms that are acceptable to Congress, because Congress has the ultimate word in this matter. And that is why H.R. 727 makes a lot of sense.

Mrs. RADEWAGEN. Thank you.

Thank you, Mr. Chairman. I yield back.

Mr. YOUNG. Resident Commissioner, you are up.

Mr. PIERLUISI. Yes. Thank you, Chairman. Listening to Governor Acevedo Vilá, and former Member of Congress, I just want to raise a question to see if you can explain to me what kind of status you envision in Puerto Rico's future? What is your specific position on status? Because I, frankly, do not get it.

And I will be respectful. You know very well the way Congress works. Congress approves bills every day we are in session that apply or not to Puerto Rico, based on its power under the territory clause of the U.S. Constitution. The Supreme Court of the United States, ever since the beginning of the 20th century, decided that Puerto Rico is an unincorporated territory, meaning that Puerto Rico could become either a state or a nation. Two choices: statehood or nationhood.

Yet we are a territory. We have our own constitution—good constitution, by the way. We are called a commonwealth. But, as you well know, that is the situation. Any day here, they can deal with us and we have no vote. We have a say, but no vote.

Now, looking at the future, what do you want Puerto Rico to be? Do you want Puerto Rico to be recognized as a sovereign nation, and then strike getting to a compact or treaty with the United States providing for the economic benefits you were talking about? Is that what you want? Or do you want Puerto Rico to continue being a territory as it is, and then keep trying to get better treatment in the laws that Congress approves on a daily basis?

Mr. VILÁ. Resident Commissioner, I just said that, for me, status quo is not the alternative, and doing nothing is not the alternative. I also said that what we need to get to is a new economic relationship which is described in many of my essays. One of them is included as an annex to my written statement.

In that sense, what I think we need to establish is a new relationship based on a compact in which we clarify the powers of Congress and we clarify the powers the people and the government of Puerto Rico will have.

To me, this is a political will situation, not a legal question. Actually, I ask any of you to look into the U.S. Constitution and read to me the clause where it talks about unincorporated territory. It is nowhere. It is nowhere. The Constitution only talks about territories.

But when the U.S. Government came to the realization that they had Puerto Rico—back then Philippines, many of the territories— but that they were not on the path toward statehood, they had a political situation. And then a new theory came to accommodate that new reality, and now we are called unincorporated territories.

But that is not in the Constitution. That is nowhere in the Constitution.

So, to me, what we need is to reach a political will for the new economic relationship. And I firmly believe that the best alternative for the people of Puerto Rico and for the United States is what we have called sovereign commonwealth, estado libre asociado soberano, where you clarify the powers of Congress, and you clarify the powers of the people of Puerto Rico. For me, the most important one has to do with economic development.

Mr. PIERLUISI. Would that be a territory, or would that be a sovereign nation in association with the United States?

Mr. VILÁ. A new relationship, the same way that, before, there were only territories, and then, after that, it was accepted to have unincorporated territories. I think what we have to reach is a political and economic agreement, and then we will deal with the legal structure.

Mr. PIERLUISI. And would Puerto Ricans continue to be American citizens——

Mr. VILÁ. Yes.

Mr. PIERLUISI [continuing]. Even if they are residing in a sovereign nation, as opposed to the United States?

Mr. VILÁ. Yes, it is a matter of political will.

Mr. YOUNG. We will continue this.

Mr. LaMalfa.

Mr. LAMALFA. Thank you, Mr. Chairman. I just had a question I wanted to throw out there on the idea of Puerto Rican bonds that might be going into bankruptcy. I am trying to work through this a little bit here, I am trying to get familiar here, but it is the possibility that previous bonds could end up in bankruptcy. What would that mean for investors? And then, what kind of confidence would anybody have in future bonds going forward?

And then, how would this lay over with how things look with Greece—how would that differ from the country of Greece, with those governments defaulting? What kind of confidence would investors be able to have with Puerto Rico at that point?

Mr. FORTUÑO. Mr. Chairman, should I give it a try?

Mr. YOUNG. He just put it out. Anybody wants to answer it——

Mr. FORTUÑO. I will be happy to, of course. And some of the members of this committee know my background. I slashed expenses by 20 percent. I am proud to be a fiscal conservative. But I can tell you that I believe that the rules in the country should apply in the same way for creditors and debtors across the country, regardless of whether you are dealing with the credit of Detroit, California, Florida, or Puerto Rico. And, in that sense, I believe that certainty is required.

Some people have stated in the past, well, if you now implement a Chapter 9, or you allow Chapter 9 to actually benefit both creditors and debtors of debt issued by Puerto Rico, you will be changing the rules of the game. That is exactly what this Congress does every day, and that is exactly what investors in every type of paper face every single day. Congress changes rules, especially tax rules, every single day.

So, in that sense, nothing special. But I strongly believe that there ought to be fiscal responsibility on the part of the territory, but there ought to be certain rules that apply to debtors and creditors. And Chapter 9 applies in the 50 states; it ought to apply across the country, including the territories.

Mr. VILÁ. May I just add that what will happen is the same thing that happened in Detroit. The same thing. You have an orderly process to deal with the situation. We are not—we are talking about municipalities or instrumentalities of the central government that might go bankrupt. So, in that sense, you have a very recent experience in Detroit. So that is the same. It is basically allowing those corporations and those instrumentalities of the government of Puerto Rico to use that tool.

And I just want to clarify also that the reason Resident Commissioner Pierluisi's bill is so important is because the local government in Puerto Rico approved a local law and was declared unconstitutional by a Federal court. That case is pending in Boston, in the First Circuit, Boston Court of Appeals. We will see what happens.

The problem is that we don't get action from Congress. And then, when the local legislature of Puerto Rico decided to somehow act, then we have a Federal court say, "You cannot do that." So I don't know of any other place in the world that doesn't have rules——

Mr. LAMALFA. And that feels like——

Mr. VILÁ [continuing]. To deal with the status——

Mr. LAMALFA [continuing]. Already, right? If the court is stopping you from doing things. But——

Mr. VILÁ. I missed you, sorry.

Mr. BARCELÓ. Can I make a statement?

Mr. LAMALFA. We don't change tax rules every day around here. We have had a package that has been very difficult to do tax reform around here, so it is not as easy as maybe it is made out to be.

But go ahead, sir.

Mr. BARCELÓ. We are very concerned. People are concerned about the bond holders, and they think of the bond holders as wealthy bond holders from the Nation, from the United States. A lot of the bond holders—and I don't know how much of a percentage, but a large percentage are poor people of Puerto Rico, retirees. And some of the retirement funds in Puerto Rico have invested heavily in Puerto Rican bonds, because they have faith in the government of Puerto Rico. So they would also be subject to not only the bond holders in Wall Street, but the individual bond holders and family bond holders in Puerto Rico will be affected by anything that is done.

And when something is done in an orderly fashion, it is the best way to do it. If nothing is done, and then the roof falls down on everyone, then everybody is going different ways, and going to court, and court proceedings for years and years and years. That is why it is being sought. Nobody expected this to ever happen.

One of the problems is that in Puerto Rico there has been a— as a colony, we have created a dependency. You have heard Governor Vilá speak about how he wants to have U.S. citizenship and not participate in the democratic process. How can anybody that says that they believe in democracy and that they want the U.S. citizenship, not want to participate in the democratic process of the nation they are citizens with? Somebody is telling a lie or does not understand what democracy is, and does not understand what U.S. citizenship means, because they want citizenship but they don't want to vote. Oh, that is bad, to have representation in the government of our Nation is prejudicial.

I mean how can that even be accepted? I wouldn't have the gall to go any place and say, "I am a Democrat, I believe in democracy, but I don't want to have the right to vote or the right to representation."

Mr. LaMalfa. Yes, I am sorry, sir.

Mr. Young. Time is up.

Mr. LaMalfa. OK, thank you. Just be careful on asking for statehood, because you might get more EPA than you ever asked for, because my resources, we can't get at in California any more due to those guys.

Mr. Young. The Ranking Member.

Mr. Sablan. Yes, on the EPA part, you get it whether you are an outlying area, you could be in Midway and get the EPA. Trust me.

[Laughter.]

Mr. Sablan. Would it be possible for the people of Puerto Rico to come together and figure this out themselves, and then come to Congress and tell us what it is you want?

I have learned in my short 7 years here in Congress that you don't ask a question unless you know the answer. If you are really going to look to Congress for guidance—seriously, is there a way for you to finally come together and——

Mr. Pierluisi. Would the gentleman yield?

Mr. Sablan. I yield to the gentleman from Puerto Rico.

Mr. Pierluisi. See, the problem, Mr. Sablan, is that as I was saying, in Alaska they held a referendum, a plebiscite, years before they came a state. And 57 percent chose statehood, and 43 percent said they didn't want it. It always happens. In Alaska—correct me if I am wrong, Mr. Chairman—but I believe there are people who still want Alaska to be independent.

[Laughter.]

Mr. Young. Primarily because of the EPA.

[Laughter.]

Mr. Pierluisi. The same happened in Texas. Texas was an independent nation before it joined the Union. So you will always have different opinions and different factions. So, to ask Puerto Ricans, "Oh, why don't you just agree, all of you," it is just an easy way out, with all due respect——

Mr. Sablan. Reclaiming my time——

Mr. Pierluisi [continuing]. Because Congress needs to act——

Mr. Sablan. Reclaiming my time. I am just suggesting—I am naive—that in Puerto Rico, just like in the Northern Mariana Islands, politics is something we discuss breakfast, lunch, and dinner.

I reclaim, Mr. Chairman, and this is interesting, I hope I didn't offend anyone. And, if I did, then that is your problem, not mine.

[Laughter.]

Mr. SABLAN. But I am enlightened. I am going through the same growing pains, although Puerto Rico has been in this since 1902— or 1908.

Mr. PIERLUISI. In 1898 we became a territory, a U.S. territory.

Mr. SABLAN. 1898. Well, see, that is what happened when that war broke out in Cuba. The United States won the war. They kept Puerto Rico and sold off to the Germans. And that is where we left off, but now I am so glad we are together again. See, it is so wonderful. The world goes around in circles. And in 100 years we will probably be down there and you are up here, because you are a state.

But I will tell you this much. There are so many times when I am trying to get something done in Congress and I pray, "If only Puerto Rico were a state, and they would be out of my way."

[Laughter.]

Mr. SABLAN. Thank you very much, Mr. Chairman, for this hearing.

Mr. VILÁ. May I react to his comment? I know it was not a question, but I think that probably we all agree.

I am going to say two things in terms of things that are happening and have been shown here. For example, Pierluisi's bill for Chapter 9 has bipartisan support in Puerto Rico, and that is very rare. So you have statehooders, pro-commonwealthers, all sectors supporting that. A coalition has been created to deal with the health issue, Medicare and Medicaid, also with bipartisan support. That is new. Probably 10 years ago that would have been impossible. That is why my presentation is basically about the economic crisis.

I think you have a responsibility and a unique opportunity. I am not talking only about Congress. It has to do also with the executive branch. This crisis is going to get complicated. And as I said, and I repeat it, we are in this together. The solution for this crisis needs the U.S. Government to come to the table and be part of that solution. I think, on that, we might also be able to get some kind of agreement beyond political parties in Puerto Rico.

Mr. YOUNG. I want to thank everybody at this table. I may have to leave here in a moment if—my Vice Chairman, because we have a vote on.

Miriam, what is—and this is for all of you—how does this tax structure work for the bigger companies that—pharmaceuticals and I don't know what else is down there. How does that work, and what benefit does it bring to Puerto Rico?

Mr. BARCELÓ. I think it hurts Puerto Rico.

Mr. YOUNG. Pardon?

Mr. BARCELÓ. I think it hurts Puerto Rico, Mr. Chairman. I think that—for a long time I have been saying that if we reduce this 90 percent tax credit to the corporations, basically the pharmaceuticals, down to 70 percent, instead of paying 4 percent they would pay 12 percent. It would mean about $3 to $4 billion more in revenues for the government of Puerto Rico, and we could start solving this economic situation.

But the incumbent now, the government, the Governor and the Popular Party, will never do that because when the campaign comes along, the lobbyists and the lawyers from these corporations, they raise a lot of money for them. And that is——

Mr. YOUNG. Well, what I am leading up to, it is just not pharmaceuticals. There are other ones. But that would bring money into the Puerto Rican economy.

Mr. BARCELÓ. Definitely, yes.

Mr. YOUNG. Because, right now, some of these companies don't even have workers from Puerto Rico, do they?

Mr. BARCELÓ. Yes, they do——

Mr. YOUNG. But Miriam—wait a minute. Miriam, go ahead.

Ms. RAMIREZ. Well, I have spent a lot of years now looking at this, because when I first started coming up here I thought it was the independentistas who were obstructing the deal. And I was bumping into these lobbyists who were actually——

Mr. YOUNG. Now, don't knock lobbyists all the time. I want you to know something. They do inform people. But I just—because you are basically all lobbyists, sitting at that table.

Ms. RAMIREZ. I realize that.

Mr. YOUNG. OK. So——

Ms. RAMIREZ. What I mean to say is that I found these pro-corporation—this particular type of corporation lobbyists interfering with the work that we were doing up here to try to convince Congress to move on this issue. And since then, the GAO has produced—I have introduced that and have links in my testimony—has produced evidence that this is one of the biggest tax evasion scams in the whole world. Almost every country is looking at this very seriously. And I have met with people in the finance—in the Ways & Means Committee, and they are very concerned about the fact that there are all these trillion—this is in the papers every day—trillion dollars of money out there in foreign countries.

But here is the problem. We are coded as foreign in the IRS. I don't know if the other territories are, but we are coded as foreign under Section 933, which is what has allowed the benefits for these people who relocated to Puerto Rico, for these corporations. And I just have the numbers from Microsoft, because they became public. But I know for a fact that this is happening also with the pharmaceuticals and everybody else. The contrast is here we are talking about how Puerto Rico is sinking in bankruptcy, how Puerto Rico—do you think the people of Puerto Rico don't see that? That is why they are leaving.

Mr. YOUNG. OK, stop right there. What I am looking for, if that is happening—because we have another bill that has been introduced by, I believe, a gentleman—Duncan, is it Duncan, South Carolina—that wants a congressional control board.

Does anybody there support that?

Mr. PIERLUISI. Mr. Chairman, would you yield?

Mr. YOUNG. I am going to, yes.

Mr. PIERLUISI. It is not a bill. He wrote a letter. And some are advocating for that. I should say for the record that I oppose that.

Mr. YOUNG. OK.

Mr. PIERLUISI. I mean Puerto Rico, as we have discussed, we have a republican form of government, a constitution blessed by this Congress.

So, unless you suspend the effectiveness of our constitution—which makes no sense—you don't appoint a financial control board to take over Puerto Rico. Puerto Rico, with all due respect to the District of Columbia, is not the District of Columbia. It is not the city of New York. We are a territory. And there is case law from the Supreme Court saying that——

Mr. YOUNG. I understand what the gentleman——

Mr. PIERLUISI [continuing]. We deserve deference, in terms of our own self-government for our local——

Mr. YOUNG. I am about ready to run out of time. But here is what I am looking for.

As you know, I am a proponent, because it is probably the central solution, and you all have a vote, just say you are going to be a state and be a state. And then that may not happen, because this is—this cannon is an awful—has a long fuse on it.

I have problems, and with the Congress. I have, like I said, been in this business for a long time and watched the attitude, which is bad. We don't need a bunch of foreigners—by the way, back in the United States—we don't need two Senators that are new. We don't need five Democrat Congressmen—which is not true, by the way, you would probably end up all being Republicans, all due respects.

[Laughter.]

Mr. YOUNG. Because I lived through that. We were all Democrats, now we are all Republican.

But I do think we have to—and my job is to try to keep this alive and moving, because somewhere we have to solve this economic problem. I personally think statehood would do it. I may be wrong.

We also have to consider the fact that maybe we change the tax laws so we can pick those up a little bit, where we can take—be more solvent. But the present system, the status quo, is not working. I said this 21 years ago, and if I am alive 20 more—God help you guys if I am alive 20 more years. But the fact is I would like to see this not be a black eye on American citizens, and Puerto Rico be accepted as equal.

I do apologize, and I want to thank the panel, we have a vote on. And for those Delegates that don't have to vote, you've got it made. You don't have to run over there and have a vote and miss a vote, you know? If you miss a vote, they say you have committed a crime.

If there are no other questions, I will adjourn.

Ms. BORDALLO. Mr. Chairman?

Mr. YOUNG. Yes, ma'am.

Ms. BORDALLO. May the territories take over this meeting?

Mr. YOUNG. Absolutely. I have offered to her [Delegate Radewagen], if she wants to do it. Are you through? OK.

We are adjourned.

[Whereupon, at 4:35 p.m., the subcommittee was adjourned.]

[ADDITIONAL MATERIALS SUBMITTED FOR THE RECORD]

[LIST OF DOCUMENTS SUBMITTED FOR THE RECORD RETAINED IN THE COMMITTEE'S OFFICIAL FILES]

—June 22, 2015, Diaspora Puerto Rico 51st State, Statement for the Record.

—June 23, 2015, Mr. Luis G. Rivera Marín, Esq. Statement for the Record.

—June 23, 2015, Dr. Gabriel J. Roman, President, Citizens Movement for Statehood, Guayama, Puerto Rico, Statement for the Record.

—June 23, 2015, The Honorable Larry Seilhamer, Minority Leader, New Progressive Party Delegation, Senate of Puerto Rico, Statement for the Record.

—June 24, 2015, Dr. Gladys Escalona de Motta, Senator José A. Ortiz-Daliot, Alliance for Free Association ALAS, Letter to Chairman Don Young.

—June 24, 2015, The Honorable Sergio E. Estevez, Municipal Legislator, Municipality of Carolina, Minority Whip Leader for the New Progressive Party, Statement for the Record.

—June 24, 2015, Dennis O. Freytes, American Patriots for Equality (Igualdad)—Civil Rights, Statement for the Record.

—June 24, 2015, Mr. Franklin D. Lopez, "The Time for Equality is Now!," Statement for the Record.

—June 24, 2015, Aníbal Acevedo Vilá, former Governor of Puerto Rico, Submission for the Record, "Supreme Court of the United States, LIMTIACO v. CAMACHO."

—June 24, 2015, Aníbal Acevedo Vilá, former Governor of Puerto Rico, Submission for the Record, "Toward the Economic Refounding of Puerto Rico and its Commonwealth Status."

○